Mighty Maxims

2021 Edition

-- By Randall Nagy

CONTENTS

Foreword

Encouraging words from famous people is a tonic. From eliminating depression to encouraging us to treat each other better, what we think about *literally* governs how we feel.

When it comes to entertainment, I believe that the preferences of countless generations of independent readers can help us sort the rubbish out from amongst the rubies.

So since greater thoughts make for a greater people, a quest for greater virtues often starts with reading the time-honored classics. -Even the tomes penned in a time when mankind understood much more about building a maintainable society, than we apparently do today.

In as much as our minds need as much (if not more!) nourishment as our bodies, I felt the need to publish a hand-selected treasure-trove of favorite quotations. I hope this collection of over 1,800 insights encourages and inspires your soul as much as they do mine.

Sharing Is Caring

Also allow me to share some free resources with you:

The first is *"Doctor Quote."* Available in both a free and paid edition, this classic quote database will run on all versions of Microsoft

Windows, as well as all versions of Linuix with a 32 bit Microsoft Windows Emulator.

Doctor Quote:
https://github.com/soft9000/DoctorQuote/tree/master/DoctorQuote32

The next is "*The Classic Scriptures*," or depending upon your tolerance for inspiration, "*The Sierra Bible*."

Why do I share Bible search programs? - Because The Bible has been called the cornerstone of Western civilization. -Studying that rock is the very reason why may begin collecting inspirational quotes:

TheBibleProjects:
https://github.com/soft9000/TheBibleProjects

I would also like to mention Project Gutenberg. A fantastic treasure trove of some of the greatest freely available works of all time, it is a marvelous resource to be aware of.

At the time of this penning, the link is:

Project Gutenberg:
https://www.gutenberg.org

No matter how great any collection of thoughts may be, reading a lot of quotations can become a tedious. If the eyes begin to tire, feel free to try some of the tips listed in the back of the book... they might put a little fun back into your inspirational quote-seeking quest!

Finally, by way of a disclaimer: I reserve the right to have a few errors here. I many not know *precisely* who said what-first and when... but I know what I like.

Mighty Maxims

Maxim #1: (Frank) Gelett Burgess

Thinking a smile all the time will keep your face youthful.

Maxim #2: A. M. Rosenthal

When something important is going on, silence is a lie.

Maxim #3: A. Poincelot

Some people think that all the world should share their misfortunes, though they do not share in the sufferings of any one else.

Maxim #4: A. W. Tozer

To be right with God has often meant to be in trouble with men.

Maxim #5: A.L. Williams

You can give in to the failure messages and be a bitter deadbeat of excuses. Or you can choose to be happy and positive and excited about life.

Maxim #6: Abigail Adams

We have too many high-sounding words, and too few actions that correspond with them.

Maxim #7: Abigail Van Buren

There are two kinds of people in the world. Those who walk into a room and say, "There you are" and those who say, "Here I am"

Maxim #8: Abraham H. Maslow

A musician must make music, an artist must paint, a poet must write, if they are to be ultimately at peace with themselves.

Maxim #9: Abraham H. Maslow

We are not in a position in which we have nothing to work with. We already have capacities, talents, direction, missions, callings.

Maxim #10: Abraham Lincoln

We must ask where we are and whither we are tending.

Maxim #11: Abraham Lincoln

What I do say is that no man is good enough to govern another man without that other's consent.

Maxim #12: Abraham Lincoln

With malice toward none, with charity for all, with firmness in the right as God gives us to see the right, let us finish the work we are in.

Maxim #13: Abraham Lincoln

When you have got an elephant by the hind legs and he is trying to run away, it's best to let him run.

Maxim #14: Abraham Lincoln

People are just about as happy as they make up their minds to be.

Maxim #15: Abraham Lincoln

There's no honorable way to kill, no gentle way to destroy. There is nothing good in war. Except its ending.

Maxim #16: Abraham Lincoln

What is conservatism? Is it not adherence to the old and tried, against the new and untried?

Maxim #17: Abraham Lincoln

People who like this sort of thing will find this the sort of thing they like.

Maxim #18: Abraham Lincoln

Towering genius disdains a beaten path.

Maxim #19: Adlai Stevenson

We can chart our future clearly and wisely only when we know the path which has led to the present.

Maxim #20: Adlai Stevenson

Understanding human needs is half the job of meeting them.

Maxim #21: Adolf Hitler

What luck for the rulers that men do not think.

Maxim #22: Aeschylus

The wisest of the wise may err.

Maxim #23: Aesop

Plodding wins the race.

Maxim #24: Aesop

Our insignificance is often the cause of our safety.

Maxim #25: African Proverb

Where there is no shame, there is no honor.

Maxim #26: Agnes Repplier

People who cannot recognize a palpable absurdity are very much in the way of civilization.

Maxim #27: Aharon Appelfeld

The writer in western civilization has become not a voice of his tribe, but of his individuality. This is a very narrow-minded situation.

Maxim #28: Al Bernstein

Success is often the result of taking a misstep in the right direction.

Maxim #29: Al Neuharth

The difference between a mountain and a molehill is your perspective.

Maxim #30: Alan Kay

The best way to predict the future is to invent it.

Maxim #31: Alan Paton

Let me not be afraid to defend the weak because of the anger of the strong, nor afraid to defend the poor because of the anger of the rich.

The only way to make sense out of change is to plunge into it, move with it, and join the dance.

The real passion of the twentieth century is servitude.

Real generosity toward the future consists in giving all to what is present.

Too many have dispensed with generosity in order to practice charity.

Truth, like light, blinds. Falsehood, on the contrary, is a beautiful twilight that enhances every object.

We call first truths those we discover after all the others.

Maxim #38: Albert Camus

Your successes and happiness are forgiven you only if you generously consent to share them.

Maxim #39: Albert Camus

Those who lack the courage will always find a philosophy to justify it.

Maxim #40: Albert Einstein

To understand the world one must not be worrying about one's self.

Maxim #41: Albert Einstein

The high destiny of the individual is to serve rather than to rule...

Maxim #42: Albert Einstein

Our task must be to free ourselves... by widening our circle of compassion to embrace all living creatures and the whole of nature and its beauty.

Maxim #43: Albert Einstein

Science without religion is lame; religion without science is blind.

Maxim #44: Albert Einstein

Though our conduct seems so very different from that of the higher animals, the primary instincts are much alike in them and in us.

Maxim #45: Albert Einstein

Try not to become a man of success but rather try to become a man of value.

Maxim #46: Albert Einstein

We can't solve problems by using the same kind of thinking we used when we created them.

Maxim #47: Albert Einstein

"If I had only known, I would have been a locksmith."

Maxim #48: Albert Einstein

To know is nothing at all; to imagine is everything.

Maxim #49: Albert Einstein

Only a life lived for others is worth living.

We cannot possibly let ourselves get frozen into regarding everyone we do not know as an absolute stranger.

The purpose of human life is to serve and show compassion and the will to help others.

Success is not the key to happiness. Happiness is the key to success. If you love what you are doing, you will be successful.

There is no higher religion than human service. To work for the common good is the greatest creed."

Sometimes only a change of viewpoint is needed to convert a tiresome duty into an interesting opportunity.

The more powerful and original a mind, the more it will incline towards the religion of solitude.

Maxim #56: Aldous Huxley

So long as men worship the Caesars and Napoleons, the Caesars and Napoleons will arise to make them miserable.

Maxim #57: Aldous Leonard Huxley

There's only one corner of the universe you can be certain of improving, and that's your own self.

Maxim #58: Aldous Leonard Huxley

That men do not learn very much from the lessons of history is the most important of all the lessons of history.

Maxim #59: Alexander Chase

The banalities of a great man pass for wit.

Maxim #60: Alexander Pope

Trust not yourself, but your defects to know, make use of every friend and every foe.

Maxim #61: Alfred A. Montapert

The main source of our wealth is goodness. The affections and the generous qualities that God admires in a world full of greed.

The chief danger in life is that you may take too many precautions.

The art of progress is to preserve order amid change.

We think in generalities, but we live in detail.

The most important function of the university in an age of reason is to protect reason from itself.

We are responsible for actions performed in response to circumstances for which we are not responsible.

The darkest day in life is the one in which we expect something for nothing.

Private passions tire and exhaust themselves, public ones never.

Maxim #69: Alvin Toffler

The illiterate of the 21st century will not be those who cannot read and write, but those who cannot learn, unlearn, and relearn.

Maxim #70: Ambrose Gwinett Bierce

There's nothing new under the sun, but there are lots of old things we don't know.

Maxim #71: Ambrose Redmoon

Courage is not the absence of fear, but rather the judgment that something else is more important than fear.

Maxim #72: American Proverb

You can't steal second base with your foot on first.

Maxim #73: American Proverb

The price of your hat isn't the measure of your brain.

Maxim #74: Amos Bronson Alcott

The less routine the more life.

You can give without loving, but you cannot love without giving.

The books that everybody admires are those that nobody reads.

To accomplish great things, we must not only act, but also dream; not only plan, but also believe.

There is no prejudice that the work of art does not finally overcome.

The quality of expectations determines the quality of our action.

The man who acquires the ability to take full possession of his own mind may take possession of anything else to which he is justly entitled.

Maxim #81: Andrew Carnegie

The way to become rich is to put all your eggs in one basket and then watch that basket.

Maxim #82: Andrew Jackson

Take time to deliberate; but when the time for action arrives, stop thinking and go in.

Maxim #83: Andrew Jackson

You must pay the price if you wish to secure the blessing.

Maxim #84: Andrew Jensen

The real acid test of courage is to be just your honest self when everybody is trying to be like somebody else.

Maxim #85: Andrew W. Mathis

It is bad luck to be superstitious.

Maxim #86: Andy Warhol

People need to be made more aware of the need to work at learning how to live because life is so quick and sometimes it goes away too quickly.

Maxim #87: Anita Brookner

She was a handsome woman of forty-five and would remain so for many years.

Maxim #88: Anna Eleanor Roosevelt

This is a strange, little, complacent country [Switzerland], in many ways a USA in miniature but of course nearer the center of disturbance!

Maxim #89: Anne Frank

Whoever is happy will make others happy too.

Maxim #90: Anne Frank

The final forming of a person's character lies in their own hands.

Maxim #91: Anne Sophie Swetchine

We reform others unconsciously when we walk uprightly.

Maxim #92: Anne W. Schaef

Sometimes it helps to know that I just can't do it all. One step at a time is all that's possible -- even when those steps are taken on the run.

Maxim #93: Anonymous

The wheel that squeaks the loudest is the first to be replaced.

Maxim #94: Anonymous

Let experience be your teacher, let challenges be the test of life.

Maxim #95: Anonymous

Death to all fanatics!

Maxim #96: Anonymous

I have read many books, but the Bible reads me.

Maxim #97: Anonymous

Quigley's Law: Whoever has any authority over you, no matter how small, will atttempt to use it.

Maxim #98: Anonymous

When your OUTGO exceeds your INCOME then your UPKEEP will be your DOWNFALL.

Maxim #99: Anonymous

The difference between goals and mission is reflected in the difference between I want to get married and I want to have a successful marriage.

It is no pleasure to build a web and catch only flies when one knows there is a wasp about.

But if a man happens to find himself ... he has a mansion which he can inhabit with dignity all the days of his life.

Often I think writing is a sheer paring away of oneself leaving always something thinner, barer, more meager.

Every accomplishment starts with the decision to try.

Anybody with money to burn will easily find someone to tend the fire.

In the land of the blind, the one-eyed man is insane.

You can't antagonize and influence at the same time.

Greediness often defeats its own ends, by making us scratch for every trifle when we should dig for gold alone.

None of us are responsible for all the things that happen to us, but we are responsible for the way we act when they do happen.

Most of us will never do great things, but we can do small things in a great way.

One nice thing about egotists: they don't talk about other people.

Don't care if you'r rich or not, as long as you can live comfortably and have everything you want.

A liberal is a socialist with a wife and two children.

You cannot achieve the impossible without attempting the absurd.

We are changed as we change our environment.

There is one way to handle the ignorant and malicious critic. Ignore him.

There are hundreds of languages in the world but a smile speaks them all.

People are more violently opposed to fur than leather because it's safer to harass rich women than motorcycle gangs.

The road to success is lined with many tempting parking spaces.

Maxim #119: Anonymous

Thinking is only a process of talking to yourself.

Maxim #120: Anonymous

Plan well before you take the journey. Remember the carpenter's rule: Measure twice, cut once.

Maxim #121: Anonymous

The kind of ancestors we have had is not as important as the kind of descendants our ancestors have.

Maxim #122: Anonymous

You can't expect to meet the challenges of today with yesterday's tools and expect to be in business tomorrow.

Maxim #123: Anonymous

When people yearn with all their hearts For just one treasure far away; They close their eyes to countless joys That crowd around them every day.

Maxim #124: Anonymous

One of society's biggest problems today is that we've allowed relationships to be accepted as impermanent, particularly marriage.

Maxim #125: Anonymous

That which we obtain too easily, we esteem too lightly.

Maxim #126: Anonymous

One of the horrors of hell is the undying memory of a misspent life.

Maxim #127: Anonymous

Without love intelligence is dangerous; without intelligence love is not enough.

Maxim #128: Anonymous

The best throw of the dice is to throw them away.

Maxim #129: Anonymous

Success goes to your head, failure to your heart.

Maxim #130: Anonymous

The first 90 percent of the task takes 90 percent of the time, the last 10 percent takes the other 90 percent.

The first impression one gets of a new ruler and his brains is from seeing the men he has chosen to have around him.

Success is the proper utilization of failure.

Value friendship for what there is in it, not for what can be gotten out of it.

The trick is to hold opinions without letting opinions hold you.

True prosperity is the result of well-placed confidence in ourselves and our fellow man.

The future lies before you, like paths of pure white snow. Be careful how you tread it, for every step will show.

There are few people more often in the wrong than those who cannot endure to be thought so.

Wise are they who have learned these truths: Trouble is temporary. Time is a tonic. Tribulation is a test tube.

You make a living by what you get, but you make a life by what you give.

The dogs bark but the caravan moves on.

The price of peace is righteousness.

Thinking things has been done through the ages; knowing things remains to be done.

Maxim #143: Anonymous

The well being of the people is the supreme law.

Maxim #144: Anonymous

Some people grin and bear it; others smile and do it.

Maxim #145: Anonymous

People are attracted to happy people.

Maxim #146: Anonymous

We are not primarily on this earth to see through one another, but to see one another through.

Maxim #147: Anonymous

The first step of handling anything is gaining an ability to face it.

Maxim #148: Anonymous

Technology does not drive change -- it enables change.

Maxim #149: Anonymous

People who like others are people others like.

What man does not understand, he fears; and what he fears, he tends to destroy.

They say an elephant never forgets, but what's he got to remember?

You can't steal second base and keep your foot on first.

When spring is dancing among the hills, one should not stay in a little dark corner.

Some people forget to plant in the spring, idle away the summer hours and then expect to reap in the fall.

What on earth are you doing for Heaven's sake?

You're not what you think you are; you're not what others think you are; you're what you think others think you are!

Your happiness is intertwined with your outlook on life.

We did not inherit the land from our forefathers-we are borrowing it from our children.

Preserve the old, but know the new.

People fail many times, but they become failures only when they begin to blame someone else.

Without wind, grass does not move.

There is no freedom without the power to defend it.

Maxim #163: Anonymous

You can tell what a man is by what he does when he hasn't anything to do.

Maxim #164: Anonymous

Opportunities are often missed because we are broadcasting when we should be listening.

Maxim #165: Anonymous

Profits are an opinion, cash is a fact.

Maxim #166: Anonymous

When the going seems easy, you may be going downhill.

Maxim #167: Anonymous

Remember that your failures are the seeds of your most glorious successes. Be sad if you must, but don't despair.

Maxim #168: Anonymous

Today's progress was yesterday's plan.

Maxim #169: Anonymous

To believe is to be strong. Doubt cramps energy. Belief is power.

When you go out to buy, don't show your silver.

People should know what you stand for. They should also know what you won't stand for.

The harder you fall, the higher you bounce.

The search for the perfect venture can turn into procrastination. Your idea may or may not have merit. The key is to get started.

Whatever your lot in life, build something on it.

Secular education can make men clever, but it cannot make them good.

We are all friends at heart. We just need more tragedies to prove it to ourselves.

True happiness comes from doing what's right not just doing what makes you feel good.

The shortest distance between two people is laughter.

Trust can be a powerful weapon.

Successful leaders have the courage to take action where others hesitate.

Taxes are not levied for the benefit of the taxed.

The Ten Commandments are not multiple choice

The essence of life is taking over.

When we are right we can afford to keep our tempers. When we are wrong, we can't afford not to.

The biggest step you can take is the one you take when you meet the other person halfway.

People will do tomorrow what they did today because that is what they did yesterday.

Then went the Pharisees, and took counsel how they might entangle him in his talk.

What's so remarkable about Love at first sight? It's when people have been looking at each other for years that it becomes remarkable.

The best way to get and keep good people is to give them room to grow.

Remember, people will judge you by your actions, not your intentions. You may have a heart of gold - but so does a hard-boiled egg.

There is nothing as cheap and weak in debate as assertion that is not backed by facts.

The secret to happiness is not in doing what one likes to do, but in liking what one has to do.

People who run down others are taking a roundabout way of praising themselves.

Real leaders are ordinary people with extraordinary determination.

People will laugh at you, but let not that prevent you.

The most effective answer to an insult is silence.

Somewhere, something incredible is waiting to be known.

The best defense against logic is ignorance.

There's no such thing as a dangerous weapon, only dangerous men.

The best way to knock the chip off your neighbor's shoulder is to pat him on the back.

The smallest good deed is better than the grandest intention.

The best teacher is the person who gets others to teach. We learn when we teach.

You become like those who you idealize, admire and follow.

What is true for you is what you have observed yourself.

Prejudice is being down on something you're not up on.

When two quarrel, both are in the wrong.

You can't do it, unless you dream it, first!

To keep your friends treat them kindly; to kill them, treat them often.

Solitude is the despair of fools, the torment of the wicked, and the joy of the good.

You're on the road to success when you realize that failure is only a detour.

"I'm prepared for all emergencies but totally unprepared for everyday life."

The way to learn is to begin.

When you go home, Tell them of us, and say For your tomorrow, We gave our today.

What men learn from history is that men do not learn from history.

Think of what others ought to be like, then start being like that yourself.

The finest eloquence is that which gets things done.

Real courage is when you know you're licked before you begin, but you begin anyway and see it through no matter what.

Maxim #218: Anonymous

Maxim #218: Anonymous

Practice random kindness and senseless acts of beauty.

Maxim #219: Anonymous

There is no teaching force like a good man's life.

Maxim #220: Anonymous

To do great, important tasks, two things are necessary: a plan and not quite enough time.

Maxim #221: Anonymous

The real danger is not that computers will begin to think like men, but that men will being to think like computers.

Maxim #222: Anonymous

You will have many friends when you use a corkscrew.

Maxim #223: Anonymous

Prayer moves the hand that moves the universe.

Maxim #224: Anonymous

Shaw's Principle: Build a system that even a fool can use, and only a fool will want to use it.

There is nothing wrong with making mistakes. Just don't respond with errors.

Truth comes only to a prepared mind.

The two hardest things to handle in life are failure & success.

Where ambition ends happiness begins.

Worry: a sustained form of fear caused by indecision.

Remember: the average is as close to the bottom as it is to the top.

Opportunities always look bigger going than coming.

Peace won by the compromise of principles is a short-lived achievement.

Yesterday is a canceled check; tomorrow is a promissory note; today is the only cash you have. Spend it wisely.

We make a living by what we get; we make a life by what we give.

The race is not always to the swift but to those who keep on running.

Your persistence is your measure of faith in yourself.

"Drawing on my fine command of language, I said nothing."

Promise only what you can deliver. Then deliver more than you promise.

The history of the world is the record of man in quest of his daily bread and butter.

The first draught a man drinks ought to be for thirst, the second for nourishment, the third for pleasure, the fourth for madness.

You cannot sit on the road to success for if you do, you will get run over.

Time invested in improving ourselves cuts down on time wasted in disapproving of others.

We all leave footprints in the sand, the question is, will we be a big heal, or a great soul.

The major justification for a life is the happiness and reward it brings to other lives.

The broad general rule is that a man is about as big as the things that make him angry.

People who do things that count, never stop to count them.

Without health you cannot enjoy wealth or happiness.

Remember, we all stumble, every one of us.

Our favorite attitude should be gratitude

You love what you find time to do.

Start with what is right rather than what is acceptable.

Think highly of yourself, for the world takes you at your own estimate.

Success comes in cans, failure in can'ts.

Set Your Goals High Enough To Inspire You And Low Enough To Encourage You.

Try to become the kind of person that people are anxious to see you as, and after you leave, they will have a lot of thinking to do.

Success does not come to those who wait... and it does not wait for anyone to come to it.

Religion is like holding on to a rock in the middle of a raging river; faith is learning how to swim.

Maxim #258: Anonymous

Some lies are so well disguised to resemble truth, that we should be poor judges of the truth not to believe them.

Maxim #259: Anonymous

Think all you speak, but speak not all you think.

Maxim #260: Anonymous

You have the power to think what you want. No matter what the circumstance.

Maxim #261: Anonymous

There are no traffic jams when you go the extra mile.

Maxim #262: Anonymous

Pain is inevitable. Suffering is optional.

Maxim #263: Anonymous

The difference between perseverance and obstinacy is that one often comes from a strong will, and the other from a strong won't.

Maxim #264: Anonymous

Forgiveness requires Repentance. Repentance requires Remorse. Remorse requires Restoration, and promising to never do it again.

Maxim #265: Anonymous

A user interface is like a joke: if you have to explain it, it's not that good.

Maxim #266: Anouk Aimee

You can only perceive real beauty in a person as they get older.

Maxim #267: Anthony J. D'Angelo

Smile, it is the key that fits the lock of everybody's heart.

Maxim #268: Anthony J. D'Angelo

Thoughts come through people, not from them.

Maxim #269: Anthony J. D'Angelo

Without a sense of caring, there can be no sense of community.

Maxim #270: Anthony J. D'Angelo

Run to meet the future or it's going to run you down.

Maxim #271: Anthony Robbins

We will act consistently with our view of who we truly are, whether that view is accurate or not.

There's no abiding success without commitment.

People are not lazy. They simply have impotent goals -- that is, goals that do not inspire them.

The quality of your life is the quality of your relationships.

Only those who have learned the power of sincere and selfless contribution experience life's deepest joy: true fulfillment.

They are best dressed, whose dress no one observes.

The most useful piece of learning for the uses of life is to unlearn what is untrue.

Pardon is the choicest flower of victory.

Reality is neither good nor bad; it just is.

Probable impossibilities are to be preferred to improbable possibilities.

There is no great genius without a mixture of madness.

The true end of tragedy is to purify the passions.

The aim of the wise is not to secure pleasure, but to avoid pain.

The secret to humor is surprise.

Those that know, do. Those that understand, teach.

One of the true tests of leadership is the ability to recognize a problem before it becomes an emergency.

The fewer the facts, the stronger the opinion.

Winning is nice if you don't lose your integrity in the process.

The four stages of man are infancy, childhood, adolescence and obsolescence.

You've got to get to the stage in life where going for it is more important than winning or losing.

If you improve or tinker with something long enough, eventually it will break or malfunction.

Maxim #292: Arthur C. Clarke

The only real problem in life is what to do next.

Maxim #293: Arthur Hugh Clough

The highest political buzz word is not liberty, equality, fraternity or solidarity; it is service.

Maxim #294: Arthur Koestler

The principal mark of genius is not perfection but originality, the opening of new frontiers.

Maxim #295: Arthur M. Schlesinger Jr.

Troubles impending always seem worse than troubles surmounted, but this does not prove that they really are.

Maxim #296: Arthur Rimbaud

What a life! True life is elsewhere. We are not in the world.

Maxim #297: Arthur Schopenhauer

Suffering by nature or chance never seems so painful as suffering inflicted on us by the arbitrary will of another.

Maxim #298: Arthur Schopenhauer

Will minus intellect constitutes vulgarity.

Wicked thoughts and worthless efforts gradually set their mark on the face, especially the eyes.

The notes I handle no better than many pianists. But the pauses between the notes --ah, that is where the art resides.

What you keep to yourself you lose, what you give away, you keep forever.

Wealth is the product of man's capacity to think.

Time mends all, ends all things earthly.

The wise man does at once what the fool does finally.

True knowledge lies in knowing how to live.

Stop worrying about the potholes in the road and celebrate the journey!

Patience is the ability to idle your motor when you feel like stripping your gears.

The real winners in life are the people who look at every situation with an expectation that they can make it work or make it better.

Egotism -- usually just a case of mistaken nonentity.

The most important thing in life is not the triumph but the struggle. The essential thing is not to have conquered but to have fought well.

To disagree, one doesn't have to be disagreeable.

Maxim #312: Barry Munro

I judge the relative strength of a man by how envious they become, of others, who enjoy a measure of success.

Maxim #313: Battista Mantuanus

We are all mad at some time or another.

Maxim #314: Ben Hecht

Hollywood held this double lure for me, tremendous sums of money for work that required no more effort than a game of pinochle.

Maxim #315: Ben Herbster

The greatest waste in the world is the difference between what we are and what we could become.

Maxim #316: Ben Kenobi

Who's more foolish? The fool, or the one who follows him?

Maxim #317: Ben Stein

The indispensable first step to getting the things you want out of life is this: Decide what you want.

Maxim #318: Ben Stein

Personal relationships are the fertile soil from which all advancement, all success, all achievement in real life grows.

Maxim #319: Ben Weininger

We must have the courage to allow a little disorder in our lives.

Maxim #320: Benjamin Disraeli

The secret of success is consistency of purpose.

Maxim #321: Benjamin Disraeli

Property has its duties as well as its rights.

Maxim #322: Benjamin Disraeli

There can be no economy where there is no efficiency.

Maxim #323: Benjamin Disraeli

The secret to success is constancy to purpose.

Maxim #324: Benjamin Franklin

Dost thou love life? Then waste not time, for time is the stuff that life is made of.

Maxim #325: Benjamin Franklin

Lying rides upon debt's back.

Maxim #326: Benjamin Franklin

Would you persuade, speak of interest, not of reason.

Maxim #327: Benjamin Franklin

Who is rich? He that rejoices in his portion.

Maxim #328: Benjamin Franklin

There are no gains without pains.

Maxim #329: Benjamin Franklin

The absent are never without fault, nor the present without excuses.

Maxim #330: Benjamin Franklin

The use of money is all the advantage there is in having money.

Maxim #331: Benjamin Franklin

Remember that time is money.

Maxim #332: Benjamin Franklin

Those who would give up essential Liberty, to purchase a little temporary Safety, deserve neither Liberty nor Safety.

Maxim #333: Benjamin Franklin

They who give up essential liberty to obtain a little temporary safety deserve neither liberty nor safety.

Maxim #334: Benjamin Franklin

Those who love deeply never grow old; they may die of old age, but they die young.

Maxim #335: Benjamin Franklin

The best tranquilizer is a clear conscience.

Maxim #336: Benjamin Franklin

We are taxed twice as much by our idleness, three times as much by our pride and four times as much by our foolishness.

Maxim #337: Benjamin Franklin

We are more heavily taxed by our idleness, pride and folly than we are taxed by government.

Maxim #338: Benjamin Franklin

One today is worth two tomorrows.

Maxim #339: Benjamin Franklin

Who is wise? He that learns from everyone. Who is powerful? He that governs his passions. Who is rich? He who is content. Who is that? Nobody.

Maxim #340: Benjamin Franklin

They that can give up essential liberty to obtain a little temporary safety deserve neither liberty nor safety.

Maxim #341: Benjamin Franklin

The secret of success is constancy to purpose.

Maxim #342: Benjamin Jowett

The way to get things done is not to mind who gets the credit for doing them.

Maxim #343: Bernadette Devlin

To gain that worth having, it may be necessary to lose everything else.

The greatest blessing of our democracy is freedom. But in the last analysis, our only freedom is the freedom to discipline ourselves.

Poverty makes you sad as well as wise.

Right is its own defense.

Happiness is not best achieved by those who seek it directly.

The time you enjoy wasting is not wasted time.

The whole problem with the world is that fools and fanatics are always so certain of themselves, but wiser people so full of doubts.

Out of compassion I destroy the darkness of their ignorance. From within them I light the lamp of wisdom and dispel all darkness from their lives.

Your motive in working should be to set others, by your example, on the path of duty.

Stay me with flagons, comfort me with apples: for I am sick of love. [The Song Of Solomon 2:5]

But I say to you, that every one who looks on a woman to lust for her has committed adultery with her already in his heart. [Matthew 5:28]

The fear of the Lord is the beginning of knowledge, but fools despise wisdom and instruction. [King Solomon]

What doth it profit a man if he gains the who world and loses his own soul?

Some friends play at friendship, but a true friend sticks closer than one's nearest kin. [Proverbs 18:24]

Maxim #357: Bible

Prove all things, hold fast to that which is true.

Maxim #358: Bible

Weeping may endure for a night, but joy comet in the morning. [Psalms 30:5]

Maxim #359: Bible

Perseverance must finish its work so that you may be mature and complete, not lacking anything. [James 1:4]

Maxim #360: Bill Clinton

Pessimism is an excuse for not trying and a guarantee to a personal failure.

Maxim #361: Bill Cosby

There is no labor a person does that is undignified; if they do it right.

Maxim #362: Bill Murray

To people who want to be rich and famous, I'd say, "Get rich first and see if that doesn't cover it."

Maxim #363: Blaise Pascal

Evil is easy, and has infinite forms.

The heart has reasons which reason knows nothing of.

When we are in love we seem to ourselves quite different from what we were before.

We know the truth, not only by the reason, but by the heart.

The property of power is to protect.

The best way to help poor people is to not be one of them.

Your true value depends entirely on what you are compared with.

The wisest man is generally he who thinks himself the least so.

Maxim #371: Bonewitz

Understanding brings control.

Maxim #372: Booker T. Washington

There are two ways of exerting one's strength; one is pushing down, the other is pulling up.

Maxim #373: Brian Corby

We may not be able to offer long-term employment, but we should try to offer long-term employability.

Maxim #374: Brian Klemmer

Practice, practice, practice until you eventually get numb on rejections.

Maxim #375: Brian Tracy

Your greatest asset is your earning ability. Your greatest resource is your time.

Maxim #376: Brian Tracy

Whatever you dwell on in the conscious grows in your experience.

Maxim #377: Bruce Barton

The essential element in personal magnetism is a consuming sincerity - an overwhelming faith in the importance of the work one has to do.

The way is not in the sky. The way is in the heart.

There is nothing so disobedient as an undisciplined mind, and there is nothing so obedient as a disciplined mind.

Through zeal, knowledge is gotten; through lack of zeal, knowledge is lost.

You yourself, as much as anybody in the entire universe, deserve your love and affection.

What you shouldn't do... Don't carry a grudge. While you're carrying the grudge, the other guy's out dancing.

What is worse than evil? The inability to bear it.

Perfecting is our destiny, but perfection never our lot.

The smaller the function, the greater the management.

The real problem is not why some pious, humble, believing people suffer, but why some do not.

The nation which forgets its defenders will be itself forgotten.

The heart of the wise man lies quiet like limpid water.

To know how to disguise is the knowledge of kings.

The most terrifying thing is to accept oneself completely.

Your vision will become clear only when you can look into your own heart. Who looks outside, dreams; who looks inside, awakens.

Our country, right or wrong. When right to be kept right; when wrong, to be put right.

To secure peace is to prepare for war.

The goal of yesterday will be the starting point of tomorrow.

Oppression can only survive through silence.

Some people change their ways when they see the light; others when they feel the heat.

Maxim #397: Changing Times

You never know what makes some people tick until they begin to unwind.

Maxim #398: Charles 'Chic' Thompson

The best way to get great ideas is to get lots of ideas and throw the bad ones away.

Maxim #399: Charles Buxton

You must never find time for anything. If you want time you must make it.

Maxim #400: Charles Caleb Colton

Commerce flourishes by circumstances, precarious, transitory, contingent, almost as the winds and waves that bring it to our shores.

Maxim #401: Charles Caleb Colton

War kills men, and men deplore the loss; but war also crushes bad principles and tyrants, and so saves societies.

Maxim #402: Charles Caleb Colton

Our income are like our shoes; if too small, they gall and pinch us; but if too large, they cause us to stumble and trip.

Maxim #403: Charles Caleb Colton

The excess of our youth are checks written against our age and they are payable with interest thirty years later.

Maxim #404: Charles Dickens

Reflect upon your present blessings, of which every man has plenty; not on your past misfortunes, of which all men have some.

Maxim #405: Charles Edward Montague

War hath no fury like a non-combatant.

Maxim #406: Charles Edwin Markham

We have committed the Golden Rule to memory. Let us now commit it to life.

Maxim #407: Charles F. Kettering

A person must have a certain amount of intelligent ignorance to get anywhere.

Maxim #408: Charles Franklin Kettering

Take good care of your future because that's where you're going to spend the rest of your life.

Maxim #409: Charles H. Parkhurst

Science has not solved problems, only shifted the points of problems.

Maxim #410: Charles Haddon Spurgeon

Trials teach us what we are; they dig up the soil, and let us see what we are made of.

Maxim #411: Charles Horton Cooley

There is hardly any one so insignificant that he does not seem imposing to some one at some time.

Maxim #412: Charles James Fox

He that is conscious of guilt cannot bear the innocence of others: So they will try to reduce all others to their own level.

Maxim #413: Charles Lynch

You can't be a winner and be afraid to lose.

Maxim #414: Charles M. Schwab

We are all salesmen every day of our lives. We are selling our ideas, our plans, our enthusiasms to those with whom we come in contact.

The man who has done his best has done everything.

Ones reputation is like a shadow, it is gigantic when it precedes you, and a pigmy in proportion when it follows.

Information travels more surely to those with a lesser need to know.

The absent are like children, helpless to defend themselves.

Profit is the ignition system of our economic engine.

The deterioration of every government begins with the decay of the principles on which it was founded.

Maxim #421: Charlotte Perkins Gilman

To attain happiness in another world we need only to believe something, while to secure it in this world we must do something.

Maxim #422: Chilton

Prefer a loss to a dishonest gain; the one brings pain at the moment, the other for all time.

Maxim #423: Chinese Proverb

All people are your relatives, therefore expect only trouble from them.

Maxim #424: Chinese Proverb

With true friends... even water drunk together is sweet enough.

Maxim #425: Chinese Proverb

Tell me, I'll forget. Show me, I may remember. But involve me and I'll understand.

Maxim #426: Chinese Proverb

When planning for a year, plant corn. When planning for a decade, plant trees. When planning for life, train and educate people.

The greatest conqueror is he who overcomes the enemy without a blow.

Patience is power. With time and patience, the mulberry leaf becomes silk.

When we have nothing to worry about we are not doing much, and not doing much may supply us with plenty of future worries.

One never needs their humor as much as when they argue with a fool.

The glory is not in never falling, but in rising every time you fall.

The man who strikes first admits that his ideas have given out.

Maxim #433: Chinese Proverb

The great question is not whether you have failed, but whether you are content with failure.

Maxim #434: Christian Nevell Bovee

The beauty seen, is partly in him who sees it.

Maxim #435: Clarence Darrow

I never wanted to see anybody die, but there are a few obituary notices I have read with pleasure.

Maxim #436: Clarence Darrow

You can only be free if I am free.

Maxim #437: Clarence Darrow

The man who fights for his fellow-man is a better man than the one who fights for himself.

Maxim #438: Clarence Darrow

Some day I hope to write a book where the royalties will pay for the copies I give away.

Maxim #439: Claude D. Pepper

The mistake a lot of politicians make is in forgetting they've been appointed and thinking they've been anointed.

Maxim #440: Clint Eastwood

Respect your efforts, respect yourself. Self-respect leads to self-discipline. When you have both firmly under your belt, that's real power.

Maxim #441: Clint Eastwood

Sometimes if you want to see a change for the better, you have to take things into your own hands.

Maxim #442: Collette

What a wonderful life I've had! I only wish I'd realized it sooner.

Maxim #443: Colton

Vice stings us even in our pleasures, but virtue consoles us, even in our pains.

Maxim #444: Confucius

It is better to light one small candle than to curse the darkness.

Maxim #445: Confucius

When we see men of a contrary character, we should turn inwards and examine ourselves.

Maxim #446: Confucius

To understand yourself is the key to wisdom.

What the superior person seeks is in themselves. What the mean person seeks is in others.

You judge yourself by what you think you can achieve, others judge you by what have achieved.

The essence of knowledge is, having it, to apply it; not having it, to confess your ignorance.

To see and listen to the wicked is already the beginning of wickedness.

When you have faults, do not fear to abandon them.

Real knowledge is to know the extent of one's ignorance.

Maxim #453: Count Leo Nikolaevich Tolstoy

The more is given the less the people will work for themselves, and the less they work the more their poverty will increase.

Maxim #454: Count Leo Nikolaevich Tolstoy

The sole meaning of life is to serve humanity.

Maxim #455: Cyndi Craven

There's a wonder in the way we're always free / To change the world by changing how we see.

Maxim #456: Cyril Connolly

Words today are like the shells and rope of seaweed which a child brings home glistening from the beach and which in an hour have lost their luster.

Maxim #457: Cyril Connolly

The friendships which last are those wherein each friend respects the other's dignity to the point of not really wanting anything from him.

Maxim #458: Cyril Connolly

The one way to get thin is to re-establish a purpose in life.

Maxim #459: Cyrus H. K Curtis

There are two kinds of men who never amount to much -- those who cannot do what they are told and those who can do nothing else.

Maxim #460: Dagobert D. Runes

Work is man's most natural form of relaxation.

Maxim #461: Daisaku Ikeda

With love and patience, nothing is impossible.

Maxim #462: Dalai Lama

Our prime purpose in this life is to help others. And if you can't help them, at least don't hurt them.

Maxim #463: Dale Carnegie

Any fool can criticize, condemn and complain - and most do.

Maxim #464: Dale Carnegie

You can conquer almost any fear if you will only make up your mind to do so. For remember, fear doesn't exist anywhere except in the mind.

Maxim #465: Dale Carnegie

Remember happiness doesn't depend upon who you are or what you have; it depends solely on what you think.

Maxim #466: Dale Carnegie

We all have possibilities we don't know about. We can do things we don't even dream we can do.

Maxim #467: Dan Brent Burt

When things are difficult, remember if it wasn't difficult everyone would be doing it. Difficulties are what make us great.

Maxim #468: Dan James

The Golden Rule of sales is the Golden Rule.

Maxim #469: Dan Mckinnon

Remember your past mistakes just long enough to profit by them.

Maxim #470: Daniel Defoe

The height of human wisdom is... to make a calm within, under the weight of the greatest storm without.

Maxim #471: Daniel Webster

There is nothing so powerful as truth, - and often nothing so strange.

Maxim #472: Danish Proverb

Unworthy offspring brag the most about their worthy descendants.

Maxim #473: David Grayson

We fail far more often by timidity than by over-daring.

Maxim #474: David Letterman

I'm just trying to make a smudge on the collective unconscious.

Maxim #475: David Mamet

We respond to a drama to that extent to which it corresponds to our dream life.

Maxim #476: David McCord

Your life will be rich for others only as it is rich for you.

Maxim #477: David McKay

The secret of success is doing well the job close at hand.

What you think about when you don't have to think, shows what you really are.

There is no real excellence in all this world which can be separated from right living.

Trust in your preparation.

Remember that a government big enough to give you everything you want is also big enough to take away everything you have.

What is originality? Undetected plagiarism.

There are two kinds of fools: One says, "This is old therefore it is good." The other one says, "This is new therefore it is better."

The proper time to influence the character of a child is about a hundred years before he is born.

Nothing is more important than reconnecting with your bliss. Nothing is as rich. Nothing is more real.

The way you think, the way you behave, the way you eat, can influence your life by 30 to 50 years.

To remind a man of the good turns you have done him is very much like a reproach.

Losers live in the past. Winners learn from the past and enjoy working in the present toward the future.

Success in life comes not from holding a good hand, but in playing a poor hand well.

Time And health are two precious assets that we don't recognize and appreciate until they have been depleted.

Time is an equal opportunity employer. Each human being has exactly the same number of hours and minutes in a day.

To establish true self-esteem we must concentrate on our successes and forget about the failures and the negatives in our lives.

You must understand that seeing is believing, but also know that believing is seeing.

The most splendid achievement of all is the constant striving to surpass yourself and to be worthy of your own approval.

The business that considers itself immune to the necessity for advertising sooner or later finds itself immune to business.

You can't just sit there and wait for people to give you that golden dream. You've got to get out there and make it happen for yourself.

Maxim #497: Diane Feinstein

That man proved his worth who can make us listen when he is by, and think when he has gone.

Maxim #498: Dianne Feinstein

You have to learn the rules of the game. And then you have to play better than anyone else.

Maxim #499: Diogenes

The sun too penetrates into privies, but is not polluted by them.

Maxim #500: Diogenes of Sinope

The art of being a slave is to rule one's master.

Maxim #501: Dolly Parton

You'd be surprised how much it costs to look this cheap.

Maxim #502: Don Herold

Unhappiness is not knowing what we want, and killing ourselves to get it.

Maxim #503: Don Marquis

Successful people are the ones who think up things for the rest of the world to keep busy at.

To be great one must be positive and gain strength from your opponents.

We are what and where we are because we have first imagined it.

The only place success comes before work is in the dictionary.

Some people obtain fame, others deserve it.

Until you make peace with who you are, you'll never be content with what you have.

If a child lives with approval, he learns to live with himself.

They sicken of the calm, who know the storm.

Maxim #511: Dorothy Serrity

We need to change so we can remain the same.

Maxim #512: Dottie Walters

Success is not a doorway, it's a staircase.

Maxim #513: Doug Horton

We are all serving a life sentence, and good behavior is our only hope for a pardon.

Maxim #514: Doug Horton

We may not always get what we want, but surely we will get what we deserve.

Maxim #515: Douglas Jerrold

Talk to him of Jacob's ladder, and he would ask the number of the steps.

Maxim #516: Douglas MacArthur

The best luck of all is the luck you make for yourself.

Maxim #517: Douglas MacArthur

Years may wrinkle the skin, but to give up interest wrinkles the soul.

Maxim #518: Douglas MacArthur

There's no security on this earth, only opportunity.

Maxim #519: Dr. Albert Schweitzer

Truth has not special time of its own. Its hour is now - always and indeed then most truly when it seems unsuitable to actual circumstances.

Maxim #520: Dr. David Viscott

To love and be loved is to feel the sun from both sides.

Maxim #521: Dr. Frank Cody

The development of desirable traits and characteristics that intangible something which we style personality - is the chief work of the school.

Maxim #522: Dr. John Gall

Systems tend to grow, and as they grow, they encroach.

Maxim #523: Dr. Jonas Edward Salk

The reward for work well done is the opportunity to do more.

Maxim #524: Dr. Loretta Scott

We can't help everyone, but everyone can help someone.

Maxim #525: Dr. Paul Williamson

"Avoid revolution or expect to get shot. Mother and I will grieve, but we will gladly buy a dinner for the National Guardsman who shot you."

Maxim #526: Dr. Robert Anthony

If you don't change your beliefs, your life will be like this forever. Is that good news?

Maxim #527: Dr. Robert Anthony

You were placed on this earth to create, not to compete.

Maxim #528: Dr. Robert Anthony

The opposite of bravery is not cowardice but conformity.

Maxim #529: Dr. Samuel Johnson

Our desires always increase with our possessions. The knowledge that something remains yet unenjoyed impairs our enjoyment of the good before us.

Maxim #530: Dr. Samuel Johnson

Praise, like gold and diamonds, owes its value to its scarcity.

Maxim #531: Dr. Samuel Johnson

The true art of memory is the art of attention.

Maxim #532: Dr. Samuel Johnson

What we hope ever to do with ease, we must learn first to do with diligence.

Maxim #533: Dr. Samuel Johnson

Sir, are you so grossly ignorant of human nature, as not to know that a man may be very sincere in good principles, without having good practice?

Maxim #534: Dr. William Osler

The clean tongue, the clear head, and the bright eye are birthrights of each day.

Maxim #535: Dryden

Self-defense is nature's oldest law.

Maxim #536: Duc de La Rochefoucauld

Perfect valor is to do unwitnessed what we should be capable of doing before all the world.

The smallest good deed is better than the grandest good intention.

Some people wanted champagne and caviar when they should have had beer and hot dogs.

There is one thing about being President, no one can tell you when to sit down.

Though force can protect in emergency, only justice, fairness, consideration and cooperation can finally lead men to the dawn of eternal peace.

Unlike presidential administrations, problems rarely have terminal dates.

Our economy is the result of millions of decisions we all make every day about producing, earning, saving, investing, and spending.

The best morale exist when you never hear the word mentioned. When you hear a lot of talk about it, it's usually lousy.

What counts is not necessarily the size of the dog in the fight; it's the size of the fight in the dog.

The only sense that is common in the long run, is the sense of change--and we all instinctively avoid it.

The end never really justifies the meanness.

Reason is a whore, surviving by simulation, versatility, and shamelessness.

So, Two cheers for Democracy: one because it admits variety and two because it permits criticism.

Am I motivated by what I really want out of life - or am I mass-motivated?

You become what you think about.

We can let circumstances rule us, or we can take charge and rule our lives from within.

Wherever there is danger, there lurks opportunity; whenever there is opportunity, there lurks danger. The two are inseparable. They go together.

Success is the progressive realization of a worthy goal or ideal.

People are where they are because that is exactly where they really want to be -- whether they will admit that or not.

The fantastic advances in the field of electronic communication constitute a greater danger to the privacy of the individual.

Somebody figured it out -- we have 35 million laws trying to enforce Ten Commandments.

As a man handles his troubles during the day, he goes to bed at night a General, Captain or Private.

The will to win, the desire to succeed, the urge to reach your full potential... these are the keys that will unlock the door to personal excellence.

We always think every other man's job is easier than our own. The better he does it, the easier it looks.

When people hear good music, it makes them homesick for something they never had, and never will have.

The liberty of the press is most generally approved when it takes liberties with the other fellow, and leaves us alone.

Maxim #562: Edgar Watson Howe

You may easily play a joke on a man who likes to argue -- agree with him.

Maxim #563: Edgar Watson Howe

When a friend is in trouble, don't annoy him by asking if there is anything you can do. Think up something appropriate and do it.

Maxim #564: Edgar Watson Howe

One of the surprising things in this world is the respect a worthless man has for himself.

Maxim #565: Edith Warton

Another unsettling element in modern art is that common symptom of immaturity, the dread of doing what has been done before.

Maxim #566: Edmund Burke

Whenever a separation is made between liberty and justice, neither, in my opinion, is safe.

What ever disunites man from God, also disunites man from man.

Restraint and discipline and examples of virtue and justice. These are the things that form the education of the world.

Check the answer you have worked out once more -- before you tell it to anybody.

And he that strives to touch the stars, Oft stumbles at a straw.

Vexed sailors cursed the rain, for which poor shepherds prayed in vain.

The invisible thing called a Good Name is made up of the breath of numbers that speak well of you.

Maxim #573: Edward G. Bulwer-Lytton

What is past is past, there is a future left to all men who have the virtue to repent and the energy to atone.

Maxim #574: Edward G. Bulwer-Lytton

The pen is mightier than the sword.

Maxim #575: Edward Gibbon

Truth, naked, unblushing truth, the first virtue of all serious history, must be the sole recommendation of this personal narrative.

Maxim #576: Edward M. Forster

Death destroys a man, the idea of Death saves him.

Maxim #577: Edward M. Forster

There lies at the back of every creed something terrible and hard for which the worshipper may one day be required to suffer.

Maxim #578: Edward M. Forster

The final test for a novel will be our affection for it, as it is the test of our friends, and of anything else which we cannot define.

Speaking of Sir Winston Churchill: He mobilized the English language and sent it into battle.

The difference between failure and success is doing a thing nearly right and doing it exactly right.

We rise in glory as we sink in pride.

On the soft bed of luxury most kingdoms have expired.

The bottom line is in heaven.

Pity those who cannot say: Thy will be done not mine, today.

There is something that is much more scarce, something finer far, something rarer than ability. It is the ability to recognize ability.

Maxim #586: Elbert Hubbard

The only man who makes money following the races is one who does it with a broom and shovel.

Maxim #587: Elbert Hubbard

There is no failure except in no longer trying.

Maxim #588: Elbert Hubbard

The greatest mistake a man can make is to be afraid of making one.

Maxim #589: Elbert Hubbard

We awaken in others the same attitude of mind we hold toward them.

Maxim #590: Elbert Hubbard

The man who has no more problems to solve, is out of the game.

Maxim #591: Eleanor Roosevelt

You always admire what you really don't understand.

Maxim #592: Eleanor Roosevelt

You have to accept whatever comes and the only important thing is that you meet it with the best you have to give.

Maxim #593: Eleanor Roosevelt

When you cease to make a contribution, you begin to die.

Maxim #594: Elizabeth Bowen

Some people are molded by their admirations, others by their hostilities.

Maxim #595: Elizabeth Layton

There is nothing worse than being a doer with nothing to do.

Maxim #596: Ellen Key

When one paints an ideal, one does not need to limit one's imagination.

Maxim #597: Elmer Holmes Davis

This nation will remain the land of the free only so long as it is the home of the brave.

Maxim #598: Emerson

Thought is the seed of action.

Maxim #599: Emile-Auguste Chartier

There are only two kinds of scholars; those who love ideas and those who hate them.

Maxim #600: Emily Dickinson

Truth is so rare that it is delightful to tell it.

Maxim #601: Eneg

Punishment becomes ineffective after a certain point. Men become insensitive.

Maxim #602: English Proverb

The older the fiddler, the sweeter the tune.

Maxim #603: English Proverb

Poverty is not a shame, but the being ashamed of it is.

Maxim #604: English Proverb

There is but an hour a day between a good housewife and a bad one.

Maxim #605: Enoch Arnold Bennett

A first-rate organizer is never in a hurry. He is never late. He always keeps up his sleeve a margin for the unexpected.

Maxim #606: Epictetus

Covetousness like jealousy, when it has taken root, never leaves a person, but with their life. Cowardice is the dread of what will happen.

Maxim #607: Epictetus

There is only one way to happiness, and that is to cease worrying about things which are beyond the power of our will.

Maxim #608: Epictetus

Practice yourself, for heaven's sake in little things, and then proceed to greater.

Maxim #609: Epictetus

Whoever does not regard what he has as most ample wealth, is unhappy, though he be master of the world.

Maxim #610: Epictetus

Only the educated are free.

Maxim #611: Epicurus

Skillful pilots gain their reputation from storms and tempests.

Maxim #612: Epicurus

Wealth consists not in having great possessions, but in having few wants.

Maxim #613: Epicurus

The art of living well and the art of dying well are one.

Maxim #614: Eric Hoffer

The end comes when we no longer talk with ourselves. It is the end of genuine thinking and the beginning of the final loneliness.

Maxim #615: Eric Hoffer

It is a sign of a creeping inner death when we no longer can praise the living.

Maxim #616: Erich Fromm

The right to express our thoughts means something only if we are able to have thoughts of our own.

Maxim #617: Ernest Hemingway

A man can be destroyed but not defeated.

Maxim #618: Ernest Hemingway

The world is a fine place and worth fighting for.

Maxim #619: Ernest Renan

The simplest schoolboy is now familiar with facts for which Archimedes would have sacrificed his life.

Maxim #620: Estonian Proverb

The work will teach you how to do it.

Maxim #621: Ethel Barrymore

You must learn day by day, year by year, to broaden your horizon. The more things you love, the more you are interested in.

Maxim #622: Ethel Percy Andrus

The human contribution is the essential ingredient. It is only in the giving of oneself to others that we truly live.

Maxim #623: Eugene W. Smith

Passion is in all great searches and is necessary to all creative endeavors.

Maxim #624: Euripides

Events will take their course, it is no good of being angry at them; he is happiest who wisely turns them to the best account.

Maxim #625: Euripides

Second thoughts are ever wiser.

Maxim #626: Ezra Pound

The real trouble with war (modern war) is that it gives no one a chance to kill the right people.

Maxim #627: Ezra Taft Benson

Unless we do his teachings, we do not demonstrate faith in Him.

Maxim #628: F. G. 'Buck' Rodgers

Leadership is the ability of a single individual through his or her actions to motivate others to higher levels of achievement.

Maxim #629: Fairfield Osborn

We do not live to extenuate the miseries of the past nor to accept as incurable those of the present.

Maxim #630: Farrar

There is only one real failure in life that is possible, and that is, not to be true to the best one knows.

Maxim #631: Father Larry Lorenzoni

The average person thinks he isn't.

Maxim #632: Felelon

The more you say, the less people remember. The fewer the words, the greater the profit.

Maxim #633: Finley Peter Dunne

The past always looks better than it was because it isn't here.

Maxim #634: Flora Whittemore

The doors we open and close each day decide the lives we live.

Maxim #635: Florence Henderson

"I can't decide whether to commit suicide or go bowling."

Maxim #636: Florence Scovel Shinn

The game of life is a game of boomerangs. Our thoughts, deeds and words return to us sooner or later with astounding accuracy.

Maxim #637: Fran Lebowitz

You can't go around hoping that most people have sterling moral characters. The most you can hope for is that people will pretend that they do.

Maxim #638: Francesco Petrarch

Suspicion is the cancer of friendship.

Maxim #639: Francis Bacon

For what a man had rather were true he more readily believes.

Maxim #640: Francis Bacon

Who questions much, shall learn much, and retain much.

Maxim #641: Francis Bacon

Prosperity discovers vice, adversity discovers virtue.

Maxim #642: Francis Bacon

Truth comes out of error more readily than out of confusion.

Maxim #643: Francis Bacon

The mould of a man's fortune is in his own hands.

Maxim #644: Francis Bacon

The best part of beauty is that which no picture can express.

Maxim #645: Francis Bacon

The best armor is to keep out of gunshot.

Maxim #646: Francis Bacon

Read not to contradict and confute; nor to believe and take for granted; nor to find talk and discourse; but to weigh and consider.

Maxim #647: Francis Bacon

Prosperity doth best discover vice; but adversity doth best discover virtue.

Maxim #648: Francis Bowen

To become a thoroughly good man is the best prescription for keeping a sound mind and a sound body.

Maxim #649: Francis H. Bradley

The man who has ceased to fear has ceased to care.

Maxim #650: Francis Herbert Hedge

Talent is a faculty that is highly developed, but genius commands all the faculties.

Maxim #651: Francis Herbert Hedge

Sympathy with nature is part of a good person's religion.

Maxim #652: Francis Picabia

Youth doesn't reason, it acts. The old man reasons and would like to make the others act in his place.

Maxim #653: Francois de La Rochefoucauld

There is hardly a man clever enough to recognize the full extent of the evil he does.

Maxim #654: Francois de La Rochefoucauld

When we cannot find contentment in ourselves, it is useless to seek it elsewhere.

Maxim #655: Francois de La Rochefoucauld

The confidence which we have in ourselves gives birth to much of that which we have in others.

Maxim #656: Francois de La Rochefoucauld

We need greater virtues to sustain good fortune than bad.

Maxim #657: Francois de La Rochefoucauld

Perfect Valor is to do, without a witness, all that we could do before the whole world.

Maxim #658: Francois de La Rochefoucauld

Weak people cannot be sincere.

The intellect is always fooled by the heart.

We all have enough strength to bear other people's woes.

We promise according to our hopes and perform according to our fears.

The creative person is both more primitive and more cultivated, more destructive, a lot madder and a lot saner, than the average person.

Peace has its victories no less than war, but it doesn't have as many monuments to unveil.

The fellow that agrees with everything you say is either a fool or he is getting ready to skin you.

Talk ought always to run obliquely, not nose to nose with no chance of mental escape.

Wit is a weapon. Jokes are a masculine way of inflicting superiority. But humor is the pursuit of a gentle grin, usually in solitude.

Success is often just an idea away.

Professionalism is knowing how to do it, when to do it, and doing it.

When you like your work every day is a holiday.

There is no greater loan that a sympathetic ear.

The ablest man I ever met is the man you think you are.

Our true destiny is not to be ministered unto but to minister to ourselves and to our fellow men.

Maxim #673: Franklin P. Jones

Perhaps the angels who fear to tread where fools rush in used to be fools who rushed in.

Maxim #674: Franklin P. Jones

The easiest way to solve a problem is to pick an easy one.

Maxim #675: Franz Peter Schubert

Some people come into our lives, leave footprints on our hearts, and we are never the same.

Maxim #676: Frederick Chiluba

The greatest lesson we can learn from the past... is that freedom is at the core of every successful nation in the world.

Maxim #677: Frederick Delius

There is only one real happiness in life, and that is the happiness of creating.

Maxim #678: Frederick Langbridge

Two men look out through the same bars: One sees the mud, and one the stars.

The true aim of everyone who aspires to be a teacher should be, not to impart his own opinions, but to kindle minds.

There are souls in this world which have the gift of finding joy everywhere and of leaving it behind them when they go.

Skeptics are never deceived.

Without grace beauty is an unabated hook.

People always make the wolf more formidable than he is.

One meets his destiny often in the road he takes to avoid it.

When we don't have what we like, we must like what we have.

Maxim #686: Friedrich Nietzsche

I teach you the superman. Man is something to be surpassed.

Maxim #687: Friedrich Nietzsche

The growth of wisdom may be gauged exactly by the diminution of ill temper.

Maxim #688: Friedrich Nietzsche

The doer alone learneth.

Maxim #689: Friedrich Nietzsche

The growth of wisdom may be gauged accurately by the decline of ill-temper.

Maxim #690: Friedrich Nietzsche

Righteousness exalteth a nation.

Maxim #691: Fulton John Sheen

The big print giveth, and the fine print taketh away.

Maxim #692: G. B. Stern

Silent gratitude isn't much use to anyone.

Maxim #693: G. K. Nielson

Successful people are not gifted; they just work hard, then succeed on purpose.

Maxim #694: Gabriel Heatter

The only time some people work like a horse is when the boss rides them.

Maxim #695: Gary Gulbranson

God is more concerned about who you are than what you do, and He is more concerned about what you do than where you do it.

Maxim #696: Gay Hendricks

The beauty of the human mind is that any decision that is made can be unmade.

Maxim #697: Gen. Joe Stilwell

The higher a monkey climbs, the more you see of his behind.

Maxim #698: Gene Brown

Today's opportunities erase yesterday's failures.

Maxim #699: General Colin Powell

Perpetual optimism is a force multiplier.

Maxim #700: General Features Corporation

Plan ahead - it wasn't raining when Noah built the Ark.

Maxim #701: General George C. Marshall

Morale is a state of mind. It is steadfastness and courage and hope.

Maxim #702: General George S. Patton

We herd sheep, we drive cattle, we lead people. Lead me, follow me, or get out of my way.

Maxim #703: General George S. Patton

Success is how high you bounce when you hit bottom.

Maxim #704: General Norman Schwarzkopf

The truth of the matter is that you always know the right thing to do. The hard part is doing it.

Maxim #705: General Omar Nelson Bradley

Peace is our goal but preparedness is the price we must pay.

Maxim #706: Geoffrey F. Abert

The most important thing about goals is having one.

Maxim #707: Geoffrey Gaberino

The real contest is always between what you've done and what you're capable of doing. You measure yourself against yourself and nobody else.

Maxim #708: Georg C. Lichtenberg

I have remarked very clearly that I am often of one opinion when I am lying down and of another when I am standing up...

Maxim #709: Georg C. Lichtenberg

The most dangerous of all falsehoods is a slightly distorted truth.

Maxim #710: Georg C. Lichtenberg

The human tendency to regard little things as important has produced very many great things.

Maxim #711: Georg Hegel

The history of the world is none other than the progress of the consciousness of freedom.

Maxim #712: George Barrington

True patriots we; for be it understood, We left our country for our country's good.

Maxim #713: George Berkeley

What is mind? No matter. What is matter? Never mind.

Maxim #714: George Bernard Shaw

The worst sin towards our fellow creatures is not to hate them, but to be indifferent to them; that's the essence of inhumanity.

Maxim #715: George Bernard Shaw

When a thing is funny, search it for a hidden truth.

Maxim #716: George Bernard Shaw

You don't learn to hold your own in the world by standing on guard, but by attacking and getting well hammered yourself.

Maxim #717: George Bernard Shaw

There is only one religion, though there are a hundred versions of it.

Maxim #718: George Bernard Shaw

One man that has a mind and knows it, can always beat ten men who haven't and don't.

Maxim #719: George Bernard Shaw

Success does not consist in never making mistakes but in never making the same one a second time.

Maxim #720: George Bernard Shaw

We do not stop playing because we grow old; we grow old because we stop playing.

Maxim #721: George Bernard Shaw

The secret of forgiving everything is to understand nothing.

Maxim #722: George Burns

How can I die? I'm booked.

Maxim #723: George Buttrick

Prayer is not a substitute for work, thinking, watching, suffering, or giving; prayer is a support for all other efforts.

Maxim #724: George Chapman

They're only truly great who are truly good.

Maxim #725: George Cooper

Brave your storm with firm endeavor. Let your vain repinings go! Hopeful hearts will find forever Roses underneath the snow!

Maxim #726: George David, MD

Wealth is when small efforts produce big results. Poverty is when big efforts produce small results.

Maxim #727: George E. Mueller

The beginning of anxiety is the end of faith, and the beginning of true faith is the end of anxiety.

Maxim #728: George Eliot

The important work of moving the world forward does not wait to be done by perfect men.

Maxim #729: George Eliot

The strongest principle of growth lies in the human choice.

Maxim #730: George Eliot

Our deeds determine us, as much as we determine our deeds.

Our words have wings, but fly not where we would.

Our deeds still travel with us from afar, And what we have been makes us what we are.

The strongest principle of growth lies in human choice.

The sons of Judah have to choose that God may again choose them. The divine principle of our race is action, choice, resolved memory.

Success is never final and Failure never fatal. It's courage that counts.

Putting off an easy thing makes it hard, and putting off a hard one makes it impossible.

The only cure for grief is action.

Maxim #738: George Holbrook Jackson

Patience has its limits, take it too far and it's cowardice.

Maxim #739: George Holbrook Jackson

The newest books are those that never grow old.

Maxim #740: George Orwell

Whoever is winning at the moment will always seem to be invincible.

Maxim #741: George Orwell

To walk through the ruined cities of Germany is to feel an actual doubt about the continuity of civilization.

Maxim #742: George Sand

Work is not man's punishment! It is his reward and his strength, his glory and his pleasure.

Maxim #743: George Santayana

To be interested in the changing seasons is, in this middling zone, a happier state of mind than to be hopelessly in love with spring.

The loftiest edifices need the deepest foundations.

The same battle in the clouds will be known to the deaf only as lightning and to the blind only as thunder.

To knock a thing down, especially if it is cocked at an arrogant angle, is a deep delight to the blood.

Progress, far from consisting in change, depends retentiveness. Those who cannot remember the past are condemned to repeat it.

We know that a man can read Goethe or Rilke in the evening, that he can play Bach and Schubert, and go to his day's work at Auschwitz in the morning.

To know the will of God is the greatest knowledge! To do the will of God is the greatest achievement.

Let us raise a standard to which the wise and honest can repair; the rest is in the hands of God.

To err is natural; to rectify error is glory.

We should not look back unless it is to derive useful lessons from past errors, and for the purpose of profiting by dearly bought experience.

True friendship is a plant of slow growth, and must undergo and withstand the shocks of adversity, before it is entitled to the appellation.

True friendship is a plant of slow growth.

To be prepared for war is one of the most effectual means of preserving the peace.

Take care of your of your life and the Lord will take of your death.

Maxim #757: Georgia Witkin

Cultivate more joy by arranging your life so that more joy will be likely.

Maxim #758: Gerald Barzan

Ten ancient commandments lousing up the fun. Along came prosperity, and then there was none.

Maxim #759: Gerald Brenan

We are closer to the ants than to the butterflies. Very few people can endure much leisure.

Maxim #760: Gerard Groote

No age or time of life, no position or circumstance, has a monopoly on success. Any age is the right age to start doing!

Maxim #761: Gerard Groote

The farther a man knows himself to be from perfection, the nearer he is to it.

Maxim #762: Geri Weitzman

Sometimes you gotta create what you want to be a part of.

When a noble life has prepared old age, it is not decline that it reveals, but the first days of immortality.

The tragedy of machismo is that a man is never quite man enough.

There is no such thing as security. There never has been.

Too aim is not enough, you must hit!

There is no eel so small but it hopes to become a whale.

The morning hour has gold in its mouth.

Speaking comes by nature, silence by understanding.

Maxim #770: German Proverb

The best answer to anger is silence.

Maxim #771: Gil Atkinson

You are one of a kind; therefore, no one can really predict to what heights you might soar. Even you will not know until you spread your wings.

Maxim #772: Gilbert K. Chesterton

The chief object of education is not to learn things but to unlearn things.

Maxim #773: Gilbert K. Chesterton

To have a right to do a thing is not the same as to be right in doing it.

Maxim #774: Gilbert K. Chesterton

We make our friends; we make our enemies; but God makes our next door neighbor.

Maxim #775: Gilbert K. Chesterton

The most dangerous criminal now is the entirely lawless modern philosopher. Compared to him, burglars and bigamists are essentially moral men.

Maxim #776: Gilbert K. Chesterton

The way to love anything is to realize that it might be lost.

Maxim #777: Giordano Bruno

Time takes all and gives all.

Maxim #778: Giulio Andreotti

Power tires only those who do not have it.

Maxim #779: Gordon B. Hinckley

Restrain your tongues in criticism of others. It is so easy to find fault. It is so much nobler to speak constructively.

Maxim #780: Graham Greene

Our worst enemies here are not the ignorant and simple, however cruel; our worst enemies are the intelligent and corrupt.

Maxim #781: Grant Hill

Parents, they're strict on you when you're little, and you don't understand why. But as you get older, you understand and you appreciate it.

Maxim #782: Grover Cleveland

Though the people support the government; the government should not support the people.

Maxim #783: Gunter Grass

The job of a citizen is to keep his mouth open.

Success as I see it, is a result, not a goal.

This, then, is the test we must set for ourselves; not to march alone but to march in such a way that others will wish to join us.

The best preparation for tomorrow is doing your best today.

The average man does not get pleasure out of an idea because he thinks it is true; he thinks it is true because he gets pleasure out of it.

The common argument that crime is caused by poverty is a kind of slander on the poor.

Precious beyond price are good resolutions. Valuable beyond price are good feelings.

Maxim #790: H. Ross Perot

The activist is not the man who says the river is dirty. The activist is the man who cleans up the river.

Maxim #791: H. W. Arnold

The worst bankruptcy in the world is the person who has lost his enthusiasm.

Maxim #792: H.G. Wells

Our true nationality is mankind.

Maxim #793: Han Suyin

There is nothing stronger in the world than gentleness.

Maxim #794: Hannah Whitall Smith

You never get a second chance to make a good first impression.

Maxim #795: Hans Margolius

Only in quiet waters do things mirror themselves undistorted. Only in a quiet mind is adequate perception of the world.

Maxim #796: Hans Reichenbach

No statement should be believed because it is made by an authority.

The five steps in teaching an employee new skills are preparation, explanation, showing, observation and supervision.

More people would learn from their mistakes if they weren't so busy denying them.

The worst disease which can afflict executives in their work is not, as popularly supposed, alcoholism; it's egotism.

Destiny is something men select; women achieve it only by default or stupendous suffering.

Security... it's simply the recognition that changes will take place and the knowledge that you're willing to deal with whatever happens.

We must teach our children to dream with their eyes open.

We must build a new world, a far better world -- one in which the eternal dignity of man is respected.

Well, I wouldn't say that I was in the great class, but I had a great time while I was trying to be great.

I can remember when a good politician had to be 75 percent ability and 25 percent actor, but I can well see the day when the reverse could be true.

When a leader is in the Democratic Party he is a boss, and when he is in the Republican Party he is a leader.

The greatest right in the world is the right to be wrong.

When the music changes, so does the dance.

The sun, the moon and the stars would have disappeared long ago had they happened to be within the reach of predatory human hands.

Poverty keeps together more homes than it breaks up.

We relish news of our heroes, forgetting that we are extraordinary to somebody too.

I am only one; but still I am one. I cannot do everything, but still I can do something; I will not refuse to do the something I can do.

Self-pity is our worst enemy, and if we yield to it, we can never do anything wise in the world.

When we do the best we can, we never know what miracle is wrought in our life, or in the life of another.

Maxim #815: Helmut Schmidt

Whoever wants to reach a distant goal must take small steps.

Maxim #816: Henri Frederic Amiel

So long as a person is capable of self-renewal they are a living being.

Maxim #817: Henri L. Bergson

There is no greater joy than that of feeling oneself a creator. The triumph of life is expressed by creation.

Maxim #818: Henri L. Bergson

Think like a man of action, act like a man of thought.

Maxim #819: Henrik Ibsen

The majority is always wrong; the minority is rarely right.

Maxim #820: Henry Adams

You can't use tact with a Congressman. A Congressman is a hog. You must take a stick and hit him on the snout.

We like to test things... no matter how good an idea sounds, test it first.

While one person hesitates because he feels inferior, another is busy making mistakes and becoming superior.

While one person hesitates because he feels inferior, the other is busy making mistakes and becoming superior.

Things do not change, we do.

We cannot kill time without injuring eternity.

Read the best books first, or you may not have a chance to read them all.

To inherit property is not to be born -- it is to be still-born, rather.

Maxim #828: Henry Fielding

Without adversity a person hardly knows whether they are honest or not.

Maxim #829: Henry Ford

There are no big problems, there are just a lot of little problems.

Maxim #830: Henry Ford

Whether you think you can or whether you think you can't, you're right!

Maxim #831: Henry Ford

Thinking is the hardest work there is, which is the probable reason so few engage in it.

Maxim #832: Henry Ford

You take all the experience and judgment of men over 50 out of the world and there wouldn't be enough left to run it.

Maxim #833: Henry Home

The truly generous is the truly wise; and he who loves not others is unblest.

 Henry Jacobsen

Whatever your job, it is important if it is what God wants you to do.

 Henry Jacobsen

The essence of worldliness is exclusion of God.

 Henry Kissinger

The task of the leader is to get his people from where they are to where they have not been.

 Henry Parry Liddon

What we do upon some great occasion will probably depend on what we already are. What we are will be the result of previous years of self-discipline.

 Henry Van Dyke

Tact is the unsaid part of what you think; its opposite, the unthought part which you say.

 Henry Van Dyke

What you possess in the world will be found at the day of your death to belong to someone else. But what you are will be yours forever.

They are all gone into the world of light, and I alone sit lingering here.

You know I say just what I think, and nothing more and less. I cannot say one thing and mean another.

Perseverance is a great element of success. If you only knock long enough and loud enough at the gate, you are sure to wake somebody.

The greatest firmness is the greatest mercy.

Thought takes man out of servitude, into freedom.

Victories that are cheap are cheap. Those only are worth having which come as the result of hard fighting.

Troubles are often the tools by which God fashions us for better things.

The moment an ill can be patiently handled, it is disarmed of its poison, though not of its pain.

Success is full of promise till one gets it, and then it seems like a nest from which the bird has flown.

To become an able and successful man in any profession, three things are necessary, nature, study and practice.

See that each hour's feelings, and thoughts and actions are pure and true; then your life will be also.

Peace is not made at the council table or by treaties, but in the hearts of men.

The men who succeed are the efficient few. They are the few who have the ambition and will power to develop themselves.

The ultimate result of shielding men from the effects of folly, is to fill the world with fools.

You are only afraid if you are not in harmony with yourself. People are afraid because they have never owned up to themselves.

All men's gains are the fruit of venturing.

The more minimal the art, the more maximum the explanation.

We have resolved to endure the unendurable and suffer what is insufferable.

Maxim #858: Hitopadesa

Subdue fate by exerting human strength to the maximum; and if, when the effort has been made and success is not achieved, no one else can be blamed.

Maxim #859: Hitopadesa

What ever is the natural propensity of a person is hard to overcome. If a dog were made a king, he would still gnaw at his shoes laces.

Maxim #860: Hitopadesa

The people of the world having once been deceived, suspect deceit in truth itself.

Maxim #861: Hodding Carter, Jr.

There are two lasting bequests we can give our children: one is roots. The other is wings.

Maxim #862: Honore De Balzac

Power is not revealed by striking hard or often, but by striking true.

Maxim #863: Horace

In the word of no master am I bound to believe.

Maxim #864: Horace

What fugitive from his country can also escape from himself.

Maxim #865: Horace

When things are steep, remember to stay level-headed.

Maxim #866: Horace

You traverse the world in search of happiness, which is within the reach of every man. A contented mind confers it on all.

Maxim #867: Horace

One wanders to the left, another to the right. Both are equally in error, but, are seduced by different delusions.

Maxim #868: Horace

We are often deterred from crime by the disgrace of others.

Maxim #869: Horace Greeley

The darkest hour in any man's life is when he sits down to plan how to get money without earning it.

Maxim #870: Horace Mann

Scientific truth is marvelous, but moral truth is divine and whoever breathes its air and walks by its light has found the lost paradise.

Maxim #871: Horace Mann

To pity distress is but human; to relieve it is Godlike.

Maxim #872: Hosea Ballou

The oppression of any people for opinion's sake has rarely had any other effect than to fix those opinions deeper, and render them more important.

Maxim #873: Howard Zinn

We will not know unless we begin.

Maxim #874: Huang Po

When thoughts arise, then do all things arise. When thoughts vanish, then do all things vanish.

Maxim #875: Hubbell

Some people grow under responsibility, others merely swell.

The impersonal hand of government can never replace the helping hand of a neighbor.

Within our impure mind the pure one is to be found.

The contented man can be happy with what appears to be useless.

When ambition ends, happiness begins.

What an elder sees sitting; the young can't see standing.

When you were born, you cried and the world rejoiced. Live your life in such a way that when you die, the world cries and you rejoice.

The work praises the man.

Maxim #883: Irving Batcheller

Opinions that are well rooted should grow and change like a healthy tree.

Maxim #884: Irving Berlin

There's an element of truth in every idea that lasts long enough to be called corny.

Maxim #885: Irwin Corey

If we don't change direction soon, we'll end up where we're going.

Maxim #886: Isaac Asimov

Self-education is, I firmly believe, the only kind of education there is.

Maxim #887: Isaac Bashevis Singer

We know what a person thinks, not when he tells us what he thinks, but by his actions.

Maxim #888: Isaac Bashevis Singer

The greatness of art is not to find what is common but what is unique.

Maxim #889: Isaac Bashevis Singer

When you betray somebody else, you also betray yourself.

Maxim #890: Isadora Duncan

What one has not experienced one will never understand in print.

Maxim #891: Israel Salanter

Promote yourself but do not demote another.

Maxim #892: Issa

Where there are humans you'll find flies, and Buddhas.

Maxim #893: Italian Proverb

After the ship has sunk, everyone knows how she might have been saved.

Maxim #894: J. Brotherton

My riches consist not in the extent of my possessions but in the fewness of my wants.

Maxim #895: J. F. Wright

True religion is the life we live, not the creed we profess, and some day will be recognized by quality and quantity, and not by brand.

Maxim #896: J. Hawes

We are often able because we think we are able.

Maxim #897: J. Ogden Armour

There may be luck in getting a good job-but there's no luck in keeping it.

Maxim #898: J. Paul Getty

In times of rapid change, experience could be your worst enemy.

Maxim #899: J.R. 'Bob' Dobbs

You know how dumb the average guy is? Well, by definition, half of them are even dumber than that.

Maxim #900: Jack Gibb

Self-confidence is the result of a successfully survived risk.

Maxim #901: Jacques Barzun

Teaching is not a lost art, but the regard for it is a lost tradition.

Maxim #902: Jacques Benigne Bossuet

The greatest weakness of all weaknesses is to fear too much to appear weak.

Maxim #903: James A. Froude

The better one is morally the less aware they are of their virtue.

The practical effect of a belief is the real test of its soundness.

The world is before you, and you need not take it or leave it as it was when you came in.

The paradox of education is precisely this -- that as one begins to become conscious one begins to examine the society in which he is being educated.

Three-fourths of the mistakes a man makes are made because he does not really know the things he thinks he knows.

You can easily judge the character of a man by how he treats those who can do nothing for him.

A dead atheist is someone who is all dressed up with no place to go.

Maxim #910: James E. Burke

The key to why things change is the key to everything.

Maxim #911: James E. Burke

We don't grow unless we take risks. Any successful company is riddled with failures.

Maxim #912: James E. Faust

Integrity is the value we set on ourselves.

Maxim #913: James F. Hind

People want to know how much you care before they care how much you know.

Maxim #914: James G. Huneker

All men of action are dreamers.

Maxim #915: James Joyce

A nation is the same people living in the same place.

Maxim #916: James L. Davis

The further an individual is from the poorhouse, the more expert one becomes on the ghetto.

Maxim #917: James Langston Hughes

Like a welcome summer rain, humor may suddenly cleanse and cool the earth, the air and you.

Maxim #918: James Madison

The essence of Government is power; and power, lodged as it must be in human hands, will ever be liable to abuse.

Maxim #919: James R. Smith

There is nothing in the world more powerful than an idea. No weapon can destroy it; no power can conquer it except the power of another idea.

Maxim #920: James Russell Lowell

The misfortunes hardest to bear are these which never came.

Maxim #921: James Russell Lowell

Where one person shapes their life by precept and example, there are a thousand who have shaped it by impulse and circumstances.

Maxim #922: James T. Ellison

The real death of America will come when everyone is alike.

Maxim #923: Jan Glidewell

You can clutch the past so tightly to your chest that it leaves your arms too full to embrace the present.

Maxim #924: Jane Taylor

Self-denial is painful for a moment, but very agreeable in the end.

Maxim #925: Jane Wagner

Our ability to delude ourselves may be an important survival tool.

Maxim #926: Jawaharlal Nehru

The person who runs away exposes himself to that very danger more than a person who sits quietly.

Maxim #927: Jay Leno

You can't stay mad at somebody who makes you laugh.

Maxim #928: Jean Baptiste Moliere

Cover that bosom that I must not see: souls are wounded by such things.

Maxim #929: Jean Baudrillard

What is a society without a heroic dimension?

Maxim #930: Jean Claude Killy

To win you have to risk loss.

Maxim #931: Jean Cocteau

We must believe in luck. For how else can we explain the success of those we don't like?

Maxim #932: Jean Cocteau

There are truths which one can only say after having won the right to say them.

Maxim #933: Jean de La Bruyere

The spendthrift robs his heirs the miser robs himself.

Maxim #934: Jean de La Bruyere

The pleasure we feel in criticizing robs us from being moved by very beautiful things.

Maxim #935: Jean de La Bruyere

The regeneration of society is the regeneration of society by individual education.

Maxim #936: Jean de La Fontaine

In short, luck's always to blame.

Every man has a right to risk his own life for the preservation of it.

Patience is bitter, but its fruit is sweet.

With children use force with men reason; such is the natural order of things. The wise man requires no law.

Remorse sleeps during prosperity but awakes bitter consciousness during adversity.

Universal silence must be taken to imply the consent of the people.

We do not know what is really good or bad fortune.

Man is the only animal that learns by being hypocritical. He pretends to be polite and then, eventually, he becomes polite.

Maxim #944: Jean Louis Rodolphe Agassiz

The time has come when scientific truth must cease to be the property of the few-when it must be woven into the common life of the world.

Maxim #945: Jean Paul

Without God there is for mankind no purpose, no goal, no hope, only a wavering future, an eternal dread of every darkness.

Maxim #946: Jean Paul

Strong character is brought out by change, weak ones by permanence.

Maxim #947: Jean Paul Richter

Time is the chrysalis of eternity.

Maxim #948: Jean Paul Richter

Only actions give life strength; only moderation gives it charm.

Maxim #949: Jean Rostand

Truth is always served by great minds, even if they fight it.

Maxim #950: Jean Rostand

We are not naive enough to ask for pure men; we ask merely for men whose impurity does not conflict with the obligations of their job.

Maxim #951: Jean Rostand

The ideal, without doubt, varies, but its enemies, alas, are always the same.

Maxim #952: Jean Shinoda Bolen

When you recover or discover something that nourishes your soul and bring joy, care enough about yourself to make room for it in your life.

Maxim #953: Jean-Luc Picard

Things are only impossible until they're not.

Maxim #954: Jean-Paul Sartre

The poor don't know that their function in life is to exercise our generosity.

Maxim #955: Jeremy Bentham

The greatest happiness of the greatest number is the foundation of morals and legislation.

The greatest evils, are from within us; and from ourselves also we must look for the greatest good.

The acquiring of culture is the development of an avid hunger for knowledge and beauty.

We've removed the ceiling above our dreams. There are no more impossible dreams.

Your childen need your presence more than your presents.

We all have dreams. But in order to make dreams come into reality, it takes an awful lot of determination, dedication, self-discipline, and effort.

What you don't see with your eyes, don't witness with your mouth.

What soap is for the body, tears are for the soul.

We must risk going too far to discover just how far we can go.

Take care of your body. It's the only place you have to live.

Time is more value than money. You can get more money, but you cannot get more time.

Whatever good things we build end up building us.

We get paid for bringing value to the market place.

Start from wherever you are and with whatever you've got.

Without constant activity, the threats of life will soon overwhelm the values.

The more you care, the stronger you can be.

You cannot change your destination overnight, but you can change your direction overnight.

Discipline has within it the potential for creating future miracles.

Don't say, 'If I could, I would.' Say, 'If I can, I will.'

Your personal philosophy is the greatest determining factor in how your life works out.

We must all suffer one of two things: the pain of discipline or the pain of regret.

Days are expensive. When you spend a day you have one less day to spend. So make sure you spend each one wisely.

Discipline is the bridge between goals and accomplishment.

If you are not willing to risk the unusual, you will have to settle for the ordinary.

Motivation is what gets you started. Habit is what keeps you going.

Learn how to be happy with what you have while you pursue all that you want.

All leaders are readers.

What you become is far more important than what you get.

I used to blame everything outside of me for my lack of progress until I found that my problem was inside.

Maxim #984: Jim Rohn

Be fascinated instead of frustrated.

Maxim #985: Jim Rohn

Either you run the day or the day runs you.

Maxim #986: Jim Rohn

Take care of your body. It's the only place you have to live.

Maxim #987: Jim Rohn

You must be careful not to let your current appetites steal away any chance we might have for a future feast.

Maxim #988: Jim Rohn

The major key to your better future is you.

Maxim #989: Jim Rohn

Every day, stand guard at the door of your mind.

Maxim #990: Jim Rohn

Excuses are the nails used to build a house of failure.

Maxim #991: Jim Rohn

You have two choices: You can make a living, or you can design a life.

Maxim #992: Jimmy Carter

We should live our lives as though Christ were coming this afternoon.

Maxim #993: Joe Namath

When you have confidence, you can have a lot of fun. And when you have fun, you can do amazing things.

Maxim #994: Joel Barker

Vision without action is merely a dream. Action without vision just passes the time. Vision with action can change the world.

Maxim #995: Joey Lauren Adams

A genius is one who can do anything except make a living.

Maxim #996: Johann Friedrich Von Schiller

The strong man is strongest when alone.

Maxim #997: Johann Friedrich Von Schiller

The jest loses its point when he who makes it is the first to laugh.

Maxim #998: Johann Friedrich Von Schiller

Truth lives on in the midst of deception.

Maxim #999: Johann Friedrich Von Schiller

Only those who have the patience to do simple things perfectly will acquire the skill to do difficult things easily.

Maxim #1000: Johann Gottfried Von Herder

What of us lies in the hearts of others is our truest and deepest self.

Maxim #1001: Johann Kaspar Lavater

You may depend upon it that he is a good man whose intimate friends are all good, and whose enemies are decidedly bad.

Maxim #1002: Johann Kaspar Lavater

You are not very good if you are not better than your best friends imagine you to be.

Maxim #1003: Johann Sebastian Bach

There's nothing remarkable about it. All one has to do is hit the right keys at the right time and the instrument plays itself.

Maxim #1004: Johann Wolfgang Von Goethe

Unlike grown ups, children have little need to deceive themselves.

Maxim #1005: Johann Wolfgang Von Goethe

Only learn to seize good fortune, for good fortune is always here.

Maxim #1006: Johann Wolfgang Von Goethe

The destiny of any nation at any given time depends on the opinion of its young people, those under twenty-five.

Maxim #1007: Johann Wolfgang Von Goethe

The best fortune that can fall to a man is that which corrects his defects and makes up for his failings.

Maxim #1008: Johann Wolfgang Von Goethe

Those are dead even for this life who hope for no other.

Only learn to seize good fortune, for good fortune's always here.

One man's word is no man's word; we should quietly hear both sides.

What government is the best? That which teaches us to govern ourselves.

What makes people happy is activity; changing evil itself into good by power, working in a God like manner.

We are shaped and fashioned by what we love.

What is not started today is never finished tomorrow.

That which is eternal in Woman lifts us above.

Maxim #1016: Johann Wolfgang Von Goethe

The man of understanding finds everything laughable.

Maxim #1017: Johann Wolfgang Von Goethe

Who is the wisest man? He who neither knows or wishes for anything else than what happens.

Maxim #1018: Johann Wolfgang Von Goethe

The little that is completed, vanishes from the sight of one who looks forward to what is still to do.

Maxim #1019: Johann Wolfgang Von Goethe

When all is said the greatest action is to limit and isolate one's self.

Maxim #1020: Johann Wolfgang Von Goethe

The man who is born with a talent which he was meant to use finds his greatest happiness in using it.

Maxim #1021: Johann Wolfgang Von Goethe

Thinking is more interesting than knowing, but less interesting than looking.

Maxim #1022: Johann Wolfgang Von Goethe

People who think honestly and deeply have a hostile attitude towards the public.

Maxim #1023: Johann Wolfgang Von Goethe

Their is nothing so terrible as activity without insight.

Maxim #1024: Johann Wolfgang Von Goethe

What by a straight path cannot be reached by crooked ways is never won.

Maxim #1025: Johann Wolfgang Von Goethe

To hard necessity ones will and fancy must conform.

Maxim #1026: Johann Wolfgang Von Goethe

Wood burns because it has the proper stuff in it; and a man becomes famous because he has the proper stuff in him.

Maxim #1027: Johann Wolfgang Von Goethe

There is a courtesy of the heart; it is allied to love. From its springs the purest courtesy in the outward behavior.

Maxim #1028: Johann Wolfgang Von Goethe

The most happy man is he who knows how to bring into relation the end and beginning of his life.

To speak gratitude is courteous and pleasant, to enact gratitude is generous and noble, but to live gratitude is to touch Heaven.

Grief drives men to serious reflection, sharpens the understanding and softens the heart.

Fear is the foundation of most government.

The happiness of society is the end of government.

The bird of paradise alights only upon the hand that does not grasp.

The secret of happiness is something to do.

Whatever one believes to be true either is true or becomes true in one's mind.

Maxim #1036: John Ciardi

The day will happen whether or not you get up.

Maxim #1037: John D. Rockefeller

Singleness of purpose is one of the chief essentials for success in life, no matter what may be one's aim.

Maxim #1038: John Dewey

We only think when we are confronted with problems.

Maxim #1039: John Dewey

The good man is the man who, no matter how morally unworthy he has been, is moving to become better.

Maxim #1040: John Dewey

Without some goals and some efforts to reach it, no man can live.

Maxim #1041: John Dykes

Our deeds follow us, and what we have been makes us what we are.

Maxim #1042: John F. Kennedy

We would like to live as we once lived, but history will not permit it.

Those who make peaceful revolution impossible will make violent revolution inevitable.

Our growing softness, our increasing lack of physical fitness, is a menace to our security.

The ignorance of one voter in a democracy impairs the security of all.

True happiness is the full use of your powers along lines of excellence in a life affording scope.

When written in Chinese, the word "crisis" is composed of two characters -- one represents danger, and the other represents opportunity.

We have the power to make this the best generation of mankind in the history of the world - or to make it the last.

Maxim #1049: John F. Kennedy

The time to repair the roof is when the sun is shining.

Maxim #1050: John F. Kennedy

When we got into office, the thing that surprised me most was to find that things were just as bad as we'd been saying they were.

Maxim #1051: John Foster

One of the strongest characteristics of genius is the power of lighting its own fire.

Maxim #1052: John Gray

When men and women are able to respect and accept their differences then love has a chance to blossom.

Maxim #1053: John Henry Newman

To live is to change, and to be perfect is to have changed often.

Maxim #1054: John Jacob Astor

Serve the classes, live with the masses. Serve the masses, live with the classes.

Maxim #1055: John Jay Chapman

All progress is experimental.

Maxim #1056: John Jay Chapman

People who love soft methods and hate iniquity forget this, -- that reform consists in taking a bone from a dog. Philosophy will not do it.

Maxim #1057: John Keats

Poetry should be great and unobtrusive, a thing which enters into one's soul, and does not startle it or amaze it with itself, but with its subject.

Maxim #1058: John La Farge

The past, though it cannot be relived, can always be repaired.

Maxim #1059: John Lennon

Work is life, you know, and without it, there's nothing but fear and insecurity.

Maxim #1060: John Locke

Reading furnishes the mind only with materials of knowledge; it is thinking that makes what we read ours.

Parents wonder why the streams are bitter, when they themselves have poisoned the fountain.

When we have done our best, we should wait the results in peace.

The social object of skilled investment should be to defeat the dark forces of time and ignorance which envelope our future.

The avoidance of taxes is the only intellectual pursuit that still carries any reward.

The importance of money flows from it being a link between the present and the future.

Virtue that wavers is not virtue.

Peace hath her victories, no less renowned than War.

Maxim #1068: John Milton

The mind is its own place, and in itself can make heaven of hell, a hell of heaven.

Maxim #1069: John Morely

You have not converted a man because you have silenced him.

Maxim #1070: John Morely

You will find most books worth reading are worth reading twice.

Maxim #1071: John Moschitta

Learning why one great book is just like every other great book is the key to understanding literature

Maxim #1072: John P. Grier

The will to believe is perhaps the most powerful, but certainly the most dangerous human attribute.

Maxim #1073: John Paul Getty

No one can possibly achieve any real and lasting success or "get rich" in business by being a conformist.

That laughter costs too much which is purchased by the sacrifice of decency.

Time is at once the most valuable and the most perishable of all our possessions.

Industry is fortunes right hand, and frugality its left.

The quickest way to become an old dog is to stop learning new tricks.

The last act crowns the play.

The distinguishing sign of slavery is to have a price, and to be bought for it.

Quality is never an accident; it is always the result of an intelligent effort.

Maxim #1081: John Ruskin

The anger of a person who is strong, can always bide its time.

Maxim #1082: John Ruskin

The weakest among us has a gift, however seemingly trivial, which is peculiar to him and which worthily used will be a gift also to his race.

Maxim #1083: John Ruskin

What distinguishes a great artist from a weak one is first their sensibility and tenderness; second, their imagination, and third, their industry.

Maxim #1084: John Ruskin

When we build, let us think that we build for ever.

Maxim #1085: John Selden

Old friends are best. King James used to call for his old shoes; they were easiest for his feet.

Maxim #1086: John Wicker

Wealth is not in making money, but in making the man while he is making money.

Maxim #1087: John Wooden

Sports do not build character. They reveal it.

Maxim #1088: John Wooden

You can't let praise or criticism get to you. It's a weakness to get caught up in either one.

Maxim #1089: Johnny Carson

The only thing money gives you is the freedom of not worrying about money.

Maxim #1090: Jorge Luis Borges

The flattery of posterity is not worth much more than contemporary flattery, which is worth nothing.

Maxim #1091: Jose Ortega Y Gasset

Tell me what you pay attention to and I will tell you who you are.

Maxim #1092: Jose Ortega Y Gasset

The good is, like nature, an immense landscape in which man advances through centuries of exploration.

Maxim #1093: Joseph Addison

To be an atheist requires an infinitely greater measure of faith than to receive all the great truths which atheism would deny.

Maxim #1094: Joseph Addison

Thy steady temper, Portius, Can look on guilt, rebellion, fraud, and Caesar, In the calm lights of mild philosophy.

Maxim #1095: Joseph Addison

There is no greater sign of a general decay of virtue in a nation, than a want of zeal in its inhabitants for the good of their country.

Maxim #1096: Joseph Addison

When a man has been guilty of any vice or folly, the best atonement he can make for it is to warn others not to fall into the like.

Maxim #1097: Joseph Chilton Pearce

We are shaped by each other. We adjust not to the reality of a world, but to the reality of other thinkers.

Maxim #1098: Joseph Conrad

Vanity plays lurid tricks with our memory.

Maxim #1099: Joseph De Maistre

Wherever an altar is found, there civilization exists.

Some people are born mediocre, some people achieve mediocrity, and some people have mediocrity thrust upon them.

What is true by lamplight is not always true by sunlight.

The passions of the young are vices in the old.

One who has imagination without learning has wings without feet.

To teach is to learn twice.

Science is for those who learn, poetry is for those who know.

I do not dwell upon your faults. You shall not dwell upon mine.

Maxim #1107: Joseph Stalin

I consider it completely unimportant who in the party will vote, or how; but what is extraordinarily important is this - who will count the votes ...

Maxim #1108: Josh Billings

One of the rarest things that a man ever does is to do the best he can.

Maxim #1109: Josh Billings

The best way to convince a fool he is wrong is to let him have his way.

Maxim #1110: Josh Billings

The best time to hold your tongue is the time you feel you must say something or bust.

Maxim #1111: Josiah Gilbert Holland

Responsibility walks hand in hand with capacity and power.

Maxim #1112: Josiah Gilbert Holland

The soul, like the body, lives by what it feeds on.

Maxim #1113: Joyce Maynard

The word no carries a lot more meaning when spoken by a parent who also knows how to say yes.

Maxim #1114: Julie Andrews

Perseverance is failing 19 times and succeeding the 20th.

Maxim #1115: Julie Cameron

Nothing dies harder than a bad idea.

Maxim #1116: Julius Robert Oppenheimer

The optimist thinks that this is the best of all possible worlds; the pessimist knows it.

Maxim #1117: Junius

The integrity of men is to be measured by their conduct, not by their professions.

Maxim #1118: Justice Robert Jackson

The price of freedom of religion or of speech or of the press is that we must put up with, and even pay for, a good deal of rubbish.

Maxim #1119: Kahlil Gibran

To understand the heart and mind of a person, look not at what he has already achieved, but at what he aspires to do.

Maxim #1120: Kahlil Gibran

Say not, "I have found the truth," but rather, "I have found a truth.

Maxim #1121: Kahlil Gibran

You can muffle the drum, and you can loosen the strings of the lyre, but who shall command the skylark not to sing?

Maxim #1122: Kahlil Gibran

The deeper that sorrow carves into your being, the more joy you can contain.

Maxim #1123: Karl G. Maeser

The truly educated man will always speak to the understanding of the most unlearned of his audience.

Maxim #1124: Karl Marx

The production of too many useful things results in too many useless people.

Maxim #1125: Karl Raimund Popper

You cannot have a rational discussion with a man who prefers shooting you to being convinced by you.

Maxim #1126: Katarina Witt

When I go our on the ice, I just think about my skating. I forget it is a competition.

Maxim #1127: Katharine Hepburn

Without discipline, there is no life at all.

Maxim #1128: Katharine Whitehorn

The easiest way for your children to learn about money is for you not to have any.

Maxim #1129: Katherine Mansfield

Regret is an appalling waste of energy; you can't build on it; it's only good for wallowing in.

Maxim #1130: Katherine Mansfield

To work -- to work! It is such infinite delight to know that we still have the best things to do.

Maxim #1131: Katherine Mansfield

The pleasure of reading is doubled when one lives with another who shares the same books.

Maxim #1132: Kathleen Norris

There is a divinity that shapes our ends - but we can help by listening for Its voice.

Maxim #1133: John Keble

When you find yourself overpowered, as it were, by melancholy, the best way is to go out and do something kind to somebody or other.

Maxim #1134: Kenneth Hildebrand

Strong lives are motivated by dynamic purposes; lesser ones exist on wishes and inclinations.

Maxim #1135: Kevin Meyers

We were all born with wings. In times of doubt: spread them.

Maxim #1136: Kin Hubbard

There's no secret about success. Did you ever know a successful man who didn't tell you about it?

Maxim #1137: Kin Hubbard

The only way to entertain some folks is to listen to them.

Maxim #1138: King George VI

The highest of distinctions is service to others.

Maxim #1139: Kipling

Take my word for it, the silliest woman can manage a clever man, but it needs a very clever woman to manage a fool.

Maxim #1140: Kirk

Too much of anything, even love, isn't necessarily a good thing.

We are what we pretend to be, so we must be careful about what we pretend to be.

Revolutions are brought about by men, by men who think as men of action and act as men of thought.

We prefer self-government with danger to servitude in tranquility.

Opportunity does not knock, it presents itself when you beat down the door.

To always be loved one must ever be agreeable.

While conscience is our friend, all is at peace; however once it is offended, farewell to a tranquil mind.

Maxim #1147: Lady Mary Wortley Montagu

We are no more free agents than the queen of clubs when she victoriously takes prisoner the knave of hearts.

Maxim #1148: Lady Nancy Astor

It isn't the common man at all who is important; it's the uncommon man.

Maxim #1149: Lao Tse

Understanding others is knowledge, Understanding oneself is enlightenment; Conquering others is power, Conquering oneself is strength.

Maxim #1150: Lao Tse

Rule a kingdom as though you were cooking a small fish - don't overdo it.

Maxim #1151: Lao-Tzu

To know yet to think that one does not know is best; Not to know yet to think that one knows will lead to difficulty.

Maxim #1152: Lao-Tzu

Truthful words are not beautiful; beautiful words are not truthful. Good words are not persuasive; persuasive words are not good.

Maxim #1153: Latin Proverb

The Autumn of the beautiful is beautiful.

Maxim #1154: Laurence J. Peter

Some problems are so complex that you have to be highly intelligent and well informed just to be undecided about them.

Maxim #1155: Laurence Sterne

Respect for ourselves guides our morals, respect for others guides our manners.

Maxim #1156: Lazarus Long

Only a sadistic scoundrel--or a fool--tells the bald truth on social occasions.

Maxim #1157: Leanna L. Bartram

True love is when your heart and your mind are saying the same thing.

Maxim #1158: Lee Iacocca

You've got to say, "I think that if I keep working at this and want it badly enough I can have it." It's called perseverance.

Maxim #1159: Lee Salk

When it gets dark enough, you can see the stars.

Maxim #1160: Lemuel K. Washburn

To correct in ourselves what we condemn in others would remove most of the evils of life.

Maxim #1161: Leo J. Muir

There is nothing so strong as gentleness, and nothing so gentle as strength.

Maxim #1162: Leon Blum

When a woman is twenty, a child deforms her; when she is thirty, he preserves her; and when forty, he makes her young again.

Maxim #1163: Leonardo Da Vinci

The noblest pleasure is the joy of understanding.

Maxim #1164: Leroy "Satchel" Paige

What's scary in life is not what people know (or don't know), but what they know that ain't so.

Maxim #1165: Leroy Van Dyke

Success... it's what you do with what you've got.

Maxim #1166: Les Brown

If you don't program yourself, life will program you!

Maxim #1167: Les Brown

You must see your goals clearly and specifically before you can set out for them. Hold them in your mind until they become second nature.

Maxim #1168: Les Brown

Review your goals twice every day in order to be focused on achieving them.

Maxim #1169: Les Brown

You don't get in life what you want; you get in life what you are.

Maxim #1170: Les Brown

Someone's opinion of you does not have to become your reality.

Maxim #1171: Les Brown

Your level of belief in yourself will inevitably manifest itself in whatever you do.

Maxim #1172: Leslie P. Hartley

The past is a foreign country; they do things differently there.

Maxim #1173:

Who in the world am I? Ah, that's the great puzzle.

Maxim #1174:

The ability to delude yourself may be an important survival tool.

Maxim #1175:

Peace of mind is that mental condition in which you have accepted the worst.

Maxim #1176:

The best way to have a good idea is to have a lot of ideas.

Maxim #1177:

We who are liberal and progressive know that the poor are our equals in every sense except that of being equal to us.

Maxim #1178:

That's the risk you take if you change: that people you've been involved with won't like the new you. But other people who do will come along.

Maxim #1179: Liza Minnelli

Reality is something you rise above.

Maxim #1180: Lloyd Jones

The man who tries to do something and fails is infinitely better than he who tries to do nothing and succeeds.

Maxim #1181: Lord Alfred Tennyson

Sin is too stupid to see beyond itself.

Maxim #1182: Lord Alfred Tennyson

To strive, to seek, to find, and not to yield.

Maxim #1183: Lord Chesterfield

Persist and persevere, and you will find most things that are attainable, possible.

Maxim #1184: Lord Chesterfield

There is nothing that people bear more impatiently, or forgive less, than contempt: and an injury is much sooner forgotten than an insult.

Maxim #1185: Lord Mansfield

True popularity is not the popularity which is followed after, but the popularity which follows after.

If you're bored with life -- you don't get up every morning with a burning desire to do things -- you don't have enough goals.

You'll never get ahead of anyone as long as you try to get even with him.

With the first link, a chain is forged. The first speech censured, the first thought forbidden, the first freedom denied, chains us all irrevocably.

When all is said and done, success without happiness is the worst kind of failure.

The trouble with our age is all signpost and no destination.

There will come a time when you believe everything is finished. That will be the beginning.

Maxim #1192: Louis Nizer

Words of comfort, skillfully administered, are the oldest therapy known to man.

Maxim #1193: Louis Pasteur

Did you ever observe to whom the accidents happen? Chance favors only the prepared mind.

Maxim #1194: Louis XIV

There is little that can withstand a man who can conquer himself.

Maxim #1195: Louis-Ferdinand Celine

Never believe straight off in a man's unhappiness. Ask him if he can still sleep. If the answer's "yes," all's well. That is enough.

Maxim #1196: Luc De Clapiers

The fruit derived from labor is the sweetest of all pleasures.

Maxim #1197: Lucille Ball

I think knowing what you cannot do is more important than knowing what you can.

Maxim #1198: Lucius Annaeus Seneca

To wish well is part of becoming well.

Why does no one confess his sins? Because he is yet in them. It is for a man who has awoke from sleep to tell his dreams.

When a man does not know what harbor he is making for, no wind is the right wind.

Only the suppressed word is dangerous.

The noblest search is the search for excellence.

When are slides are shown in a darkened room, the instructor will require the students to take notes.

When our friends get into power, they aren't our friends anymore.

Much misconstruction and bitterness are spared to him who thinks naturally upon what he owes to others rather than what he ought to expect from them.

Maxim #1206: Madame Marie Curie

Be less curious about people and more curious about ideas.

Maxim #1207: Mahatma Gandhi

Strength does not come from physical capacity. It comes from an indomitable will.

Maxim #1208: Mahatma Gandhi

Those who know how to think need no teachers.

Maxim #1209: Maimonides

Teach thy tongue to say I do not know and thou shalt progress.

Maxim #1210: Major Kira Nerys

That's the thing about faith. If you don't have it you can't understand it. And if you do, no explanation is necessary

Maxim #1211: Mal Pancoast

The odds of hitting your target go up dramatically when you aim at it.

Maxim #1212: Malcolm S. Forbes

By the time we've made it, we've had it.

Maxim #1213: Malcolm S. Forbes

When looking back, usually I'm more sorry for the things I didn't do than for the things I shouldn't have done.

Maxim #1214: Malcolm S. Forbes

There's no way to move without making waves.

Maxim #1215: Malcolm S. Forbes

The biggest mistake people make in life is not trying to make a living at doing what they most enjoy.

Maxim #1216: Malcolm S. Forbes

The smart ones ask when they don't know. And, sometimes, when they do.

Maxim #1217: Malcolm X

Truth is on the side of the oppressed.

Maxim #1218: Malcolm X

The political philosophy of black nationalism means that the black man should control the politics and the politicians in his own community; no more.

Maxim #1219: Marcel Proust

The bonds that unite another person to our self exist only in our mind.

Maxim #1220: Marcel Proust

We are healed of a suffering only by experiencing it in full.

Maxim #1221: Marcus Aurelius

The art of living is more like that of wrestling than of dancing; the main thing is to stand firm and be ready for an unseen attack.

Maxim #1222: Marcus Aurelius

Where a man can live, he can also live well.

Maxim #1223: Marcus Aurelius Antoninus

When thou art above measure angry, bethink thee how momentary is man's life.

Maxim #1224: Marcus Aurelius Antoninus

Our wills are ours, to make them Thine.

Maxim #1225: Marcus T. Cicero

The pursuit, even of the best things, ought to be calm and tranquil.

Maxim #1226: Marcus T. Cicero

The shifts of Fortune test the reliability of friends.

Virtue is its own reward.

So near is falsehood to truth that a wise man would do well not to trust himself on the narrow edge.

To the sick, while there is life there is hope.

There is no grief which time does not lessen and soften.

To disregard what the world thinks of us is not only arrogant but utterly shameless.

Reason should direct and appetite obey.

Vivere est cogitare. To think is to live.

You complain, friend Swift, of the length of my epigrams, but you yourself write nothing. Yours are shorter.

That spot of earth has special charms for me, in which a limited income produces happiness, and moderate wealth abundance.

You will succeed best when you put the restless, anxious side of affairs out of mind, and allow the restful side to live in your thoughts.

The only thing worse than a man you can't control is a man you can.

The human heart, at whatever age, opens only to the heart that opens in return.

We teachers can only help the work going on, as servants wait upon a master.

The minute a person whose word means a great deal to others dare to take the open-hearted and courageous way, many others follow.

What a fool cannot learn he laughs at, thinking that by his laughter he shows superiority instead of latent idiocy.

The first step is the hardest.

Man was made at the end of the week's work when God was tired.

There are no people who are quite so vulgar as the over-refined.

Under certain circumstances, profanity provides a relief denied even to prayer.

Maxim #1246: Mark Twain

The only way to keep your health is to eat what you don't want, drink what you don't like and do what you'd druther not.

Maxim #1247: Mark Twain

We like a man to come right out and say what he thinks, if we agree with him.

Maxim #1248: Mark Twain

The man with a new idea is a crank until the idea succeeds.

Maxim #1249: Mark Twain

There isn't a single human characteristic that can be safely labeled as "American."

Maxim #1250: Mark Twain

There's always something about your success that displeases even your best friends.

Maxim #1251: Mark Twain

Whenever you find you are on the side of the majority, it is time to pause and reflect.

Maxim #1252: Mark Twain

There is something fascinating about science. One gets such wholesale returns of conjecture out of such a trifling investment of fact.

Maxim #1253: Mark Twain

The best way to cheer yourself up is to try to cheer somebody else up.

Maxim #1254: Mark Twain

We need not worry so much about what man descends from; it's what he descends to that shames the human race.

Maxim #1255: Mark Twain

The first time a student realizes that a little learning is a dangerous thing is when he brings home a poor report card.

Maxim #1256: Marlene Dietrich

The weak are more likely to make the strong weak than the strong are likely to make the weak strong.

Maxim #1257: Marshall Fishwick

The uncommitted life isn't worth living.

Maxim #1258: Martha Grimes

We don't know who we are until we see what we can do

Maxim #1259: Martin Luther

Where God builds a church the devil builds a chapel.

Maxim #1260: Martin Luther

Justice is a temporary thing that must at last come to an end; but the conscience is eternal and will never die.

Maxim #1261: Martin Luther

Superstition, idolatry and hypocrisy have ample wages, but the truth goes begging.

Maxim #1262: Martin Luther

People must have righteous principals in the first, and then they will not fail to perform virtuous actions.

Maxim #1263: Martin Luther King Jr.

The question is not whether we will be extremists, but what kind of extremists we will be.

Maxim #1264: Martin Luther King Jr.

There is nothing more tragic than to find an individual bogged down in the length of life, devoid of breadth.

Maxim #1265: Martin Luther King Jr.

The quality, not the longevity, of one's life is what is important.

Maxim #1266: Martin Luther King Jr.

There can be no deep disappointment where there is not deep love.

Maxim #1267: Martin Luther King Jr.

Whatever your life's work is, do it well. A man should do his job so well that the living, the dead, and the unborn could do it no better.

Maxim #1268: Martin Tupper

Pain adds rest unto pleasure, and teaches the luxury of health.

Maxim #1269: Marvin J. Ashton

You can never get enough of the things you don't need, because the things you don't need can never satisfy.

Truth is reality.

Then hail! thou noble conqueror! That, when tyranny oppressed, hewed for our fathers from the wild. A land wherein to rest.

We are tomorrow's past.

The minute you settle for less than you deserve, you get even less than you settled for.

The pain of love is the pain of being alive. It is a perpetual wound.

When you choose the lesser of two evils, always remember that it is still an evil.

To change a habit, make a conscious decision, then act out the new behavior.

Maxim #1277: May Sarton

We have to dare to be ourselves, however frightening or strange that self may prove to be.

Maxim #1278: May Sarton

There is only one real deprivation... and that is not to be able to give one's gifts to those one loves most.

Maxim #1279: Merrick Winn

Usually we never know the truth. Great men take it with them to the grave. Just a few, the truly great, have the courage to tell it before they go.

Maxim #1280: Michael E. Gerber

The five essential entrepreneurial skills for success: Concentration, Discrimination, Organization, Innovation and Communication

Maxim #1281: Michel De Saint-Pierre

An optimist may see a light where there is none, but why must the pessimist always run to blow it out?

Maxim #1282: Michel Eyquem De Montaigne

We can be knowledgeable with other men's knowledge but we cannot be wise with other men's wisdom.

Since we cannot attain unto it, let us revenge ourselves with railing against it.

The weeping of an heir is laughter in disguise.

The man who fears suffering is already suffering from what he fears.

The easy, gentle, and sloping path... is not the path of true virtue. It demands a rough and thorny road.

To be prepared is half the victory.

Tell me what company you keep and I'll tell you what you are.

What you hear repeatedly you will eventually believe.

Maxim #1290: Mikhail Strabo

Only you can hold yourself back, only you can stand in your own way. Only you can help yourself.

Maxim #1291: Millard Drexler

You can't run a business without taking risks.

Maxim #1292: Milt Barber

When you arrive at your campsite, it is full.

Maxim #1293: Miss Piggy

Only time can heal your broken heart, just as only time can heal his broken arms and legs.

Maxim #1294: Mohammed

A man's true wealth is the good he does in the world.

Maxim #1295: Mohammed

When he dies, people will say, "What property has he left behind him?" But the angels will ask, "What good deeds has he sent before him7.

Maxim #1296: Mohammed

Riches are not from abundance of worldly goods, but from a contented mind.

Maxim #1297: Mohammed

Patience is the key to contentment.

Maxim #1298: Mohandas Karamchand Gandhi

Whatever you do may seem insignificant, but it is very important that you do it.

Maxim #1299: Mohandas Karamchand Gandhi

Whenever you have truth it must be given with love, or the message and the messenger will be rejected.

Maxim #1300: Mohandas Karamchand Gandhi

Satisfaction lies in the effort, not in the attainment, full effort is full victory.

Maxim #1301: Moli'ere

There is no praise to beat the sort you can put in your pocket.

Maxim #1302: Mother Teresa

The most terrible poverty is loneliness and the feeling of being unloved.

Maxim #1303: Mother Teresa

To keep a lamp burning, we have to keep putting oil in it.

Maxim #1304: Motto

The wealth of kings is in the affections of their subjects.

Maxim #1305: Motto

Upright whether in prosperous or in critical circumstances.

Maxim #1306: Muhammad Ali

The man who views the world at 50 the same as he did at 20 has wasted 30 years of his life.

Maxim #1307: Nadine Gordimer

There is no moral authority like that of sacrifice.

Maxim #1308: Nancy Simms

Winners take chances. Like everyone else, they fear failing, but they refuse to let fear control them.

Maxim #1309: Napolean

"Give me enough medals, and I'll win any war."

Maxim #1310: Napoleon Bonaparte

The infectiousness of crime is like that of the plague.

Maxim #1311: Napoleon Bonaparte

We must laugh at man to avoid crying for him.

Maxim #1312: Napoleon Bonaparte

You may ask me for anything you like except time.

Maxim #1313: Napoleon Bonaparte

The best way to keep one's word is not to give it.

Maxim #1314: Napoleon Hill

When defeat comes, accept it as a signal that your plans are not sound, rebuild those plans, and set sail once more toward your coveted goal.

Maxim #1315: Napoleon Hill

The world has the habit of making room for the man whose actions show that he knows where he is going.

Maxim #1316: Napoleon Hill

Your real boss is the one who walks around under your hat.

Maxim #1317: Nathaniel Hawthorne

We sometimes congratulate ourselves at the moment of waking from a troubled dream; it may be so the moment after death.

Maxim #1318: Nathaniel Hawthorne

The world owes all its onward impulses to men ill at ease. The happy man inevitable confines himself within ancient limits.

Maxim #1319: Neil Postman

People in distress will sometimes prefer a problem that is familiar to a solution that is not.

Maxim #1320: Nelson DeMille

We are all pilgrims on the same journey but some pilgrims have better roadmaps.

Maxim #1321: Niccolo Machiavelli

There is no avoiding war; it can only be postponed to the advantage of others.

Maxim #1322: Nicholas Breton

Thus much for thy assurance know; a hollow friend is but a hellish foe.

Maxim #1323: Nicolas Boileau-Despreaux

Greatest fools are oft most satisfied.

Maxim #1324: Niels Henrik David Bohr

The opposite of a correct statement is a false statement. But the opposite of a profound truth may well be another profound truth.

Maxim #1325: Nikki Giovanni

There're two people in the world that are not likeable: a master and a slave.

Maxim #1326: Norman Cousins

The individual is capable of both great compassion and great indifference. He has it within his means to nourish the former and outgrow the latter.

Maxim #1327: Norwegian Proverb

The lazier a man is, the more he plans to do tomorrow.

Maxim #1328: O. W. Polen

You are what you are - and not what people think you are.

Maxim #1329: Ojibway Indian Saying

Sometimes I go about pitying myself And all the while I am being carried across the sky By beautiful clouds.

Maxim #1330: Oliver Goldsmith

Crime generally punishes itself.

Maxim #1331: Oliver Goldsmith

Persecution is a tribute the great must always pay for preeminence.

Maxim #1332: Oliver Goldsmith

Those that think must govern those that toil.

Maxim #1333: Oliver Goldsmith

Some faults are so closely allied to qualities that it is difficult to weed out the vice without eradicating the virtue.

Maxim #1334: Oliver Goldsmith

Ridicule has always been the enemy of enthusiasm, and the only worthy opponent to ridicule is success.

Maxim #1335: Oliver Goldsmith

The jests of the rich are ever successful.

Maxim #1336: Oliver Herford

Tact is to lie about others as you would have them lie about you.

Maxim #1337: Oliver Wendell Holmes

Man's mind once stretched by a new idea, never regains its original dimension.

The greatest thing in this world is not so much where we are, but in what direction we are moving.

Young men know the rules, but old men know the exceptions.

Several years before birth, advertise for a couple of parents belonging to long-lived families.

The man who is always worrying whether or not his soul would be damned generally has a soul that isn't worth a damn.

Trouble creates a capacity to handle it.

The best part of our knowledge is that which teaches us where knowledge leaves off and ignorance begins.

Luck is a matter of preparation meeting opportunity.

If you wish your merit to be known, acknowledge that of other people.

We advance on our journey only when we face our goal, when we are confident and believe we are going to win out.

Put the uncommon effort into the common task... make it large by doing it in a great way.

The hand cannot reach higher than does the heart.

There are powers inside of you which, if you could discover and use, would make of you everything you ever dreamed or imagined you could become.

The Creator has not given you a longing to do that which you have no ability to do.

Maxim #1351: Orison Swett Marden

We fail to see that we can control our own destiny; make ourselves do whatever is possible; make ourselves become whatever we long to be.

Maxim #1352: Orison Swett Marden

The glow of satisfaction which follows the consciousness of doing our level best never comes to a human being from any other experience.

Maxim #1353: Orlando A. Battista

The best inheritance a parent can give his children is a few minutes of his time each day.

Maxim #1354: Oscar Wilde

Children begin by loving their parents. After a time they judge them. Rarely, if ever, do they forgive them.

Maxim #1355: Oscar Wilde

A poet can survive anything but a misprint.

Maxim #1356: Oscar Wilde

One's past is what one is. It is the only way by which people should be judged.

Maxim #1357: Oscar Wilde

The greatest of all sins is stupidity.

Maxim #1358: Oscar Wilde

She lacks the indefinable charm of weakness.

Maxim #1359: Oscar Wilde

Twenty years of romance make a woman look like a ruin, but twenty years of marriage make her something like a public building.

Maxim #1360: Oscar Wilde

There is always something infinitely mean about other people's tragedies.

Maxim #1361: Oscar Wilde

Popularity is the only insult that has not yet been offered to Mr. Whistler.

Maxim #1362: Oscar Wilde

There is no sin except stupidity.

Maxim #1363: Oscar Wilde

Whenever people agree with me I always feel I must be wrong.

Maxim #1364: Ovid

Although they posses enough, and more than enough still they yearn for more.

Maxim #1365: Ovid

Who would have known of Hector, if Troy had been happy? The road to valor is built by adversity.

Maxim #1366: Ovid

This also -- that I live, I consider a gift of God.

Maxim #1367: Owen Felltham

There is no belittling worse than to over praise a man.

Maxim #1368: P.J. O'Rourke

There's not a woman in the book, the plot hinges on unkindness to animals, and the black characters mostly drown by Chapter 29.

Maxim #1369: P.J. O'Rourke

You can't get rid of poverty by giving people money.

Maxim #1370: Paddy Ashdown

Politics is about putting yourself in a state of grace.

Maxim #1371: Pat Riley

You have no choices about how you lose, but you do have a choice about how you come back and prepare to win again.

Maxim #1372: Pat Riley

There's always the motivation of wanting to win. Everybody has that. But a champion needs, in his attitude, a motivation above and beyond winning.

Maxim #1373: Patricia Clafford

The work will wait while you show the child the rainbow, but the rainbow won't wait while you do the work.

Maxim #1374: Patty Hansen

You create your opportunities by asking for them.

Maxim #1375: Paul Brown

You can learn a line from a win and a book from a defeat.

Maxim #1376: Paul C. Roud

The fear of death keeps us from living, not from dying.

Maxim #1377: Paul Geraldy

Young men wish; love, money and health. One day, they'll say; health, money and love.

The best education consists in immunizing people against systematic attempts at education

Serious people have few ideas. People with ideas are never serious.

Our judgments judge us, and nothing reveals us, exposes our weaknesses, more ingeniously than the attitude of pronouncing upon our fellows.

"If a camel flies, no one laughs if it doesn't get very far."

When a man gets up to speak, people listen, then look. When a woman gets up to speak, people look; then if they like what they see, they listen.

This is the way of peace: Overcome evil with good, falsehood with truth, and hatred with love.

We are that which activates the body.

A crown, if it hurts us, is not worth wearing.

Prayer puts you in touch with the infinite and prepares your mind for the finite.

Time is the scarcest resource and unless it is managed nothing else can be managed.

Quality in a service or product is not what you put into it. It is what the client or customer gets out of it.

The best way to predict the future is to create it.

Promotion should not be more important than accomplishment, or avoiding instability more important than taking the right risk.

When we argue for our limitations, we get to keep them.

Peace is no more than a dream as long as we need the comfort of the clan.

Submit to the present evil, lest a greater one befall you.

You will soon break the bow if you leave it stretched.

The opinions of men who think are always growing and changing, like living children.

Walk boldly and wisely.... There is a hand above that will help thee on.

Unless you're willing to have a go, fail miserably, and have another go, success won't happen.

We triumph without glory when we conquer without danger.

Maxim #1399: Pierre Corneille

What destroys one man preserves another.

Maxim #1400: Pierre Teilhard de Chardin

The most satisfying thing in life is to have been able to give a large part of oneself to others.

Maxim #1401: Pittacus

That state is best ordered when the wicked have no command, and the good have.

Maxim #1402: Plato

We are twice armed if we fight with faith.

Maxim #1403: Plato

When men speak ill of thee, live so as nobody may believe them.

Maxim #1404: Plato

Wealth is the parent of luxury and indolence, and poverty of meanness and viciousness, and both of discontent.

Maxim #1405: Plato

Until philosophers are kings ... cities will never cease from ill, nor the human race.

Maxim #1406: Plato

The life which is unexamined is not worth living.

Maxim #1407: Plato

Philosophy is the highest music.

Maxim #1408: Plato

Thinking is the talking of the soul with itself.

Maxim #1409: Plato

We can easily forgive a child who is afraid of the dark. The real tragedy of life is when adults are afraid of the light.

Maxim #1410: Plutarch

The wildest colts make the best horses.

Maxim #1411: Plutarch

The mind is not a vessel to be filled but a fire to be kindled.

Maxim #1412: Plutarch

The mind is not a vessel that needs filling, but wood that needs igniting.

Maxim #1413: Polybius

Those that know how to win are much more numerous than those who know how to make proper use of their victories.

Maxim #1414: Princess of Wales Diana

Whoever is in the distress can call me. I will come running wherever they are.

Maxim #1415: Proverb

It is better to run back than run the wrong way.

Maxim #1416: Proverb

Sloth is the key to poverty.

Maxim #1417: Proverb

A rich child often sits in a poor mothers lap.

Maxim #1418: Proverb

Talk well of your friends and of your enemies say nothing.

Maxim #1419: Proverb

What is a big shot except a little shot that kept on shooting.

Some who will not speak against another, in the end does them harm.

Silence implies consent.

The word that is heard perishes, but the letter that is written remains.

The charitable give out the door and God puts it back through the window.

The wise man guards against the future as if it were the present.

The eyes are not responsible when the mind does the seeing.

To confess a fault freely is the next thing to being innocent of it.

The remedy for wrongs is to forget them.

Valor grows by daring, fear by holding back.

Posterity gives every man his true value.

Wisdom thoroughly learned, will never be forgotten.

Strength of mind rests in sobriety; for this keeps your reason unclouded by passion.

To what greater inspiration and counsel can we turn than to the imperishable truth to be found in this treasure house, the Bible?

The very purpose of existence is to reconcile the glowing opinion we have of ourselves with the appalling things that other people think about us.

Success often comes to those who have the aptitude to see way down the road.

The imposition of stigma is the commonest form of violence used in democratic societies.

You must choose the thoughts and actions that will lead you on to success.

The conquering of adversity produces strength of character, forges selfconfidence, engenders self-respect, and assures success in righteous endeavor.

When you hire people who are smarter than you are, you prove you are smarter than they are.

Uncertainty and mystery are energies of life. Don't let them scare you unduly, for they keep boredom at bay and spark creativity.

Maxim #1440: R. Pocock

The land too poor for any other crop, is best for raising men.

Maxim #1441: Rabindranath Tagor

Clouds come floating into my life, no longer to carry rain or usher storm, but to add colour to my sunset sky.

Maxim #1442: Rachel Carson

Those who dwell among the beauties and mysteries of the Earth are never alone or weary of life.

Maxim #1443: Racine

What a difference there is between what we say and what we think.

Maxim #1444: Ralph Nader

There can be no daily democracy without daily citizenship.

Maxim #1445: Ralph Nader

When strangers start acting like neighbors, communities are reinvigorated.

Maxim #1446: Ralph Waldo Emerson

Love, and you shall be loved. All love is mathematically just, as much as the two sides of an algebraic equation.

Maxim #1447: Ralph Waldo Emerson

Live, let live, and help live

Maxim #1448: Ralph Waldo Emerson

Skill to do comes of doing.

Maxim #1449: Ralph Waldo Emerson

He is a good man who can receive a gift well.

Maxim #1450: Ralph Waldo Emerson

Conversation enriches the understanding; but solitude is the school of genius.

Maxim #1451: Ralph Waldo Emerson

Those who live to the future must always appear selfish to those who live to the present.

Maxim #1452: Ralph Waldo Emerson

Our strength grows out of our weakness.

Maxim #1453: Ralph Waldo Emerson

Sorrow makes us all children again-destroys all differences of intellect. The wisest know nothing.

Maxim #1454: Ralph Waldo Emerson

Our knowledge is the amassed thought and experience of innumerable minds.

Maxim #1455: Ralph Waldo Emerson

Without a rich heart, wealth is an ugly beggar.

Maxim #1456: Ralph Waldo Emerson

We are prisoners of ideas.

Maxim #1457: Ralph Waldo Emerson

There is creative reading as well as creative writing.

Maxim #1458: Ralph Waldo Emerson

The measure of a great leader, is their success in bringing everyone around to their opinion twenty years later.

Maxim #1459: Ralph Waldo Emerson

To map out a course of action and follow it to an end requires some of the same courage that a soldier needs.

The fatal trait of the times is the divorce between religion and morality.

When Nature has work to be done, she creates a genius to do it.

We aim above the mark to hit the mark.

To believe your own thought, to believe that what is true for you in your private heart is true for all men-that is genius.

The meaning of good and bad, of better and worse, is simply helping or hurting.

Weed--a plant whose virtues have yet to be discovered.

What you are thunders so loudly in my ears that I cannot hear what you say. What you do rings so loudly in my ears that I cannot hear what you say.

The profoundest thought or passion sleeps as in a mine, until an equal mind and heart finds and publishes it.

Sow a thought and you reap an action; sow an act and you reap a habit; sow a habit and you reap a character; sow a character and you reap a destiny.

The excellent is new forever.

Though we travel the world over to find the beautiful we must carry it with us or we find it not.

The blazing evidence of immortality is our dissatisfaction with any other solution.

They can conquer who believe they can.

So of cheerfulness, or a good temper, the more it is spent, the more it remains.

Tell them, dear, that if eyes were made for seeing, Then Beauty is its own excuse for being.

To be great is to be misunderstood.

Skepticism is slow suicide.

Sincerity is the highest complement you can pay,

The wise through excess of wisdom is made a fool.

The power of a man increases steadily by continuing in one direction.

The god of victory is said to be one-handed, but peace gives victory on both sides.

Maxim #1481: Ralph Waldo Emerson

The eloquent man is he who is no eloquent speaker, but who is inwardly drunk with a certain belief.

Maxim #1482: Ralph Waldo Emerson

The highest compact we can make with our fellow is - 'Let there be truth between us two forevermore.'.

Maxim #1483: Ramsey Clark

The measure of your quality as a public person, as a citizen, is the gap between what you do and what you say.

Maxim #1484: Randall Nagy

Tolerance is contagious: It's just a matter of how long you've been exposed to it.

Maxim #1485: Raoul Vaneigem

Our task is not to rediscover nature but to remake it.

Maxim #1486: Raul Armesto

The world isn't interested in the storms you encountered, but whether or not you brought in the ship.

Maxim #1487: Ray Kroc

The quality of a leader is reflected in the standards they set for themselves.

Maxim #1488: Ray Lyman Wilbur

Unless we think of others and do something for them, we miss one of the greatest sources of happiness.

Maxim #1489: Ray Prince

Work is only work if you'd rather be doing something else.

Maxim #1490: Ray Stevens

The less you know, the more you think you know, because you don't know you don't know.

Maxim #1491: Raymond Holliwell

To give your best is to receive the best.

Maxim #1492: Raymond Mortimer

Tact is the art of convincing people that they know more than you do.

Maxim #1493: Reinhold Niebuhr

Our age knows nothing but reaction, and leaps from one extreme to another.

Maxim #1494: Rev. William Paley

True fortitude of understanding consists in not suffering what we do know to be disturbed by what we do not know.

Maxim #1495: Reverend Theodore M. Hesburgh

The most important thing a father can do for his children is to love their mother.

Maxim #1496: Richard Bach

You are never given a dream without also being given the power to make it true. You may have to work for it, however.

Maxim #1497: Richard Bach

The best way to pay for a lovely moment is to enjoy it.

Maxim #1498: Richard Baker

To get rich never risk your health. For it is the truth that health is the wealth of wealth.

Maxim #1499: Richard Brinsley Sheridan

The surest way to fail is not to determine to succeed.

The mark of your ignorance is the depth of your belief in injustice and tragedy.

Few men during their lifetime come anywhere near exhausting the resources dwelling within them. There are deep wells of strength that are never used.

Only if you have been in the deepest valley, can you ever know how magnificent it is to be on the highest mountain.

Scrubbing floors and emptying bedpans has as much dignity as the Presidency.

You must never regret what might have been. The past that did not happen is as hidden from us as the future we cannot see.

Say and do something positive that will help the situation; it doesn't take any brains to complain.

Maxim #1506: Robert A. Heinlein

You live and learn. Or you don't live long.

Maxim #1507: Robert A. Heinlein

You can go wrong by being too skeptical as readily as by being too trusting.

Maxim #1508: Robert Alan

The good deed you do today For a brother or sister in need Will come back to you some day For humanity's a circle in deed.

Maxim #1509: Robert Browning

So free we seem, so fettered we are!

Maxim #1510: Robert Browning

What Youth deemed crystal, Age finds out was dew.

Maxim #1511: Robert Browning

The great mind knows the power of gentleness.

Maxim #1512: Robert Browning

What I aspired to be, And was not, comforts me.

Maxim #1513: Robert Burton

The fear of death is worse than death.

Maxim #1514: Robert Collier

Visualize this thing that you want, see it, feel it, believe in it. Make your mental blueprint, and begin to build.

Maxim #1515: Robert Collier

The first principle of success is desire -- knowing what you want. Desire is the planting of your seed.

Maxim #1516: Robert Conklin

People want riches; they need fulfillment.

Maxim #1517: Robert Coover

The narrative impulse is always with us; we couldn't imagine ourselves through a day without it.

Maxim #1518: Robert Francis Kennedy

Only those who dare to fail greatly can ever achieve greatly.

Maxim #1519: Robert H. Schuller

Courage is spelled I-N-T-E-G-R-I-T-Y.

Maxim #1520: Robert H. Schuller

Tough times never last, but tough people do.

Our greatest lack is not money for any undertaking, but rather ideas, If the ideas are good, cash will somehow flow to where it is needed.

Yes, you can be a dreamer and a doer too, if you will remove one word from your vocabulary: impossible.

You never suffer from a money problem, you always suffer from an idea problem.

You can often measure a person by the size of his dream.

Winning starts with beginning.

What great things would you attempt if you knew you could not fail.

The greatest thing in family life is to take a hint when a hint is intended-and not to take a hint when a hint isn't intended.

There is so much good in the worst of us, and so much bad in the best of us, that is behooves all of us not to talk about the rest of us.

To be what we are, and to become what we are capable of becoming, is the only end of life.

You cannot run away from weakness; you must some time fight it out or perish; and if that be so, why not now, and where you stand?

There is so much good in the worst of us, and so much bad in the best of us, that it behooves all of us not to talk about the rest of us.

The world is so full of a number of things; I am sure we should all be as happy as kings.

Maxim #1533: Robert Louis Stevenson

The saints are the sinners who keep on trying.

Maxim #1534: Robert Louis Stevenson

The price we have to pay for money is sometimes liberty.

Maxim #1535: Robert Moffat

We have all eternity to celebrate our victories, but only one short hour before sunset in which to win them.

Maxim #1536: Robert Orben

"Every morning, I get up and look through the 'Forbes' list of the richest people in America. If I'm not there, I go to work"

Maxim #1537: Robert R. Young

There can be no liberty that isn't earned.

Maxim #1538: Robert Ranke Graves

There's no money in poetry, but there's no poetry in money, either.

Maxim #1539: Robert Thibodeau

To try is all. It matters not if one succeeds or fails outwardly.

What we call luck is the inner man externalized. We make things happen to us.

The eyes see only what the mind is prepared to comprehend.

The love of truth lies at the root of much humor.

There are two rules for success... 1) Never tell everything you know.

You hit home runs not by chance but by preparation.

Let us not forget who we are. Drug abuse is a repudiation of everything America is.

We might come closer to balancing the Budget if all of us lived closer to the Commandments and the Golden Rule.

Maxim #1547: Ronald Reagan

There are no such things as limits to growth, because there are no limits on the human capacity for intelligence, imagination and wonder.

Maxim #1548: Ronald Reagan

The trouble with our liberal friends is not that they're ignorant, it's just that they know so much, that isn't so.

Maxim #1549: Rosalind Russell

When something an affliction happens to you, you either let it defeat you, or you defeat it.

Maxim #1550: Rose Pastor Stokes

Some pray to marry the man they love, my prayer will somewhat vary; I humbly pray to Heaven above that I love the man I marry.

Maxim #1551: Rudyard Kipling

Words are, of course, the most powerful drug used by mankind.

Maxim #1552: Rudyard Kipling

Take up the White Man's burden -- send forth the best ye breed -- go, bind your sons to exile to serve your captives need.

Maxim #1553: Rush Limbaugh

No nation ever taxed itself into prosperity.

Maxim #1554: Russell C. Taylor

Service opens windows in your life instead of just mirrors that always reflect yourself.

Maxim #1555: Ruth E. Renkel

Sometimes the poorest man leaves his children the richest inheritance.

Maxim #1556: Ruth Smeltzer

You have not lived a perfect day... unless you have done something for someone who will never be able to repay you.

Maxim #1557: Saadi

The best loved by God are those that are rich, yet have the humility of the poor, and those that are poor and have the magnanimity of the rich.

Maxim #1558: Saadi

The beloved of the Almighty are the rich who have the humility of the poor, and the poor who have the magnanimity of the rich.

Maxim #1559: Salman Rushdie

Our lives teach us who we are.

Maxim #1560: Salman Rushdie

One of the extraordinary things about human events is that the unthinkable becomes thinkable.

Maxim #1561: Sam Rayburn

You'll never get mixed up if you simply tell the truth. Then you don't have to remember what you have said, and you never forget what you have said.

Maxim #1562: Samuel Butler

The one serious conviction that a man should have is that nothing is to be taken too seriously.

Maxim #1563: Samuel Butler

The healthy stomach is nothing if it is not conservative. Few radicals have good digestions.

Maxim #1564: Samuel Butler

There is no mistake so great as that of being always right.

Maxim #1565: Samuel Butler

Silence is not always tact, but it is tact that is golden, not silence.

Maxim #1566: Samuel Insull

Aim for the top. There is plenty of room there. There are so few at the top it is almost lonely there.

Maxim #1567: Samuel Johnson

The wise man applauds he who he thinks most virtuous; the rest of the world applauds the wealthy.

Maxim #1568: Samuel Johnson

Wickedness is always easier than virtue, for it takes a short cut to everything.

Maxim #1569: Samuel Johnson

Where secrecy or mystery begins, vice or roguery is not far off.

Maxim #1570: Samuel Johnson

There can be no friendship without confidence, and no confidence without integrity.

Maxim #1571: Samuel Johnson

The most fatal disease of friendship is gradual decay, or dislike hourly increased by causes too slender for complaint, and too numerous for removal.

Maxim #1572: Samuel M. Shoemaker

The surest mark of a Christian is not faith, or even love, but joy.

Maxim #1573: Samuel Rogers

The good are better made by ill, As odors crush'd are sweeter still.

Maxim #1574: Samuel Smiles

The duty of helping one's self in the highest sense involves the helping of one's neighbors.

Maxim #1575: Samuel Smiles

The shortest way to do many things at once is to do them one at a time.

Maxim #1576: Samuel Taylor Coleridge

Plagiarists are always suspicious of being stolen from.

Maxim #1577: Samurai Maxim

The angry man will defeat himself in battle as well as in life.

Maxim #1578: Sankara Acharya

Wisdom is not acquired save as the result of investigation.

Maxim #1579: Sarah Josepha (Buell) Hale

We need not power or splendor, Wide halls or lordly dome; The good, the true, the tender- These form the wealth of home.

Maxim #1580: Saul David Alinsky

Power is not only what you have but what the enemy thinks you have.

Study is the scourge of boyhood, the environment of youth, the indulgence of adults and the curative for the aged.

No pillows so soft as God's Promise.

With a definite, step-by-step plan -- ah, what a difference it makes! You cannot fail, because each step carries you along to the next, like a track.

Someone stole my heart. I haven't gotten it back, because I haven't found anyone to steal it back for me.

You can't rely just on talent to win.

When the cup is full, carry it even.

The greatest remedy for anger is delay.

Maxim #1588: Seneca

The courts of kings are full of people, but empty of friends.

Maxim #1589: Seneca

The fates lead the willing, and drag the unwilling.

Maxim #1590: Seneca

The mind is a matter over every kind of fortune; itself acts in both ways, being the cause of its own happiness and misery.

Maxim #1591: Seneca

We are more often frightened than hurt; and we suffer more from imagination than from reality.

Maxim #1592: Shakespeare

There's not one wise man among twenty will praise himself.

Maxim #1593: Shakespeare

What's gone, and what's past help, should be past grief.

Maxim #1594: Shakespeare

Whilst thou livest keep a good tongue in thy head.

Maxim #1595: Shall Sinha

Every single moment of your life you must choose from a number of alternatives. What you choose determines where you will end up.

Maxim #1596: Sharon Anthony Bower

People can refute your facts, but never your feelings.

Maxim #1597: Shirley Chisholm

You don't make progress by standing on the sidelines, whimpering and complaining. You make progress by implementing ideas.

Maxim #1598: Sidney Dark

The men who have gone before us have taught us how to live and how to die. We are the heirs of the ages.

Maxim #1599: Sidney J. Harris

The time to relax is when you don't have time for it.

Maxim #1600: Sidonie Gabrielle Colette

You will do foolish things, but do them with enthusiasm.

Maxim #1601: Sigmund Freud

The most complicated achievements of thought are possible without the assistance of consciousness.

Maxim #1602: Sigmund Freud

Thought is action in rehearsal.

Maxim #1603: Simone De Beauvoir

One's life has value so long as one attributes value to the life of others, by means of love, friendship, indignation and compassion.

Maxim #1604: Sir Arthur Conan Doyle

How often have I said to you that when you have eliminated the impossible, whatever remains, however improbable, must be the truth.

Maxim #1605: Sir Arthur Conan Doyle

When the impossibility has been eliminated, whatever remains, no matter how improbable... is possible.

Maxim #1606: Sir Arthur Helps

Wise sayings often fall on barren ground; but a kind word is never thrown away.

Maxim #1607: Sir Charles Higham

We are 90% alike, all we peoples, and 10% different. The trouble is that we forget the 90% and remember the 10% when we criticize others.

Maxim #1608: Sir Edwin Arnold

Pity makes the world soft to the weak and noble to the strong.

Maxim #1609: Sir Isaac Newton

This most beautiful system [The Universe] could only proceed from the dominion of an intelligent and powerful Being.

Maxim #1610: Sir James M. Barrie

The life of every person is like a diary in which he means to write one story, and writes another.

Maxim #1611: Sir John Buchan

Without humility there can be no humanity.

Maxim #1612: Sir John Lubbock

Our duty is to believe that for which we have sufficient evidence, and to suspend our judgment when we have not.

Maxim #1613: Sir John Vanbrugh

The want of a thing is perplexing enough, but the possession of it, is intolerable.

Maxim #1614: Sir John Vanbrugh

Virtue is its own reward. There's a pleasure in doing good which sufficiently pays itself.

Maxim #1615: Sir Roger Bannister

The man who can drive himself further once the effort gets painful is the man who will win.

Maxim #1616: Sir Thomas Browne

Be able to be alone. Lose not the advantage of solitude. .. but delight to be alone and single with Omnipresency....

Maxim #1617: Sir Thomas Fowell Buxton

With ordinary talents and extraordinary perseverance, all things are attainable.

Maxim #1618: Sir Thomas More

They have no lawyers among them, for they consider them as a sort of people whose profession it is to disguise matters.

The employer generally gets the employees he deserves.

So the heart be right, it is no matter which way the head lieth. [Executed by beheading.]

There never will exist anything permanently noble and excellent in the character which is a stranger to resolute self-denial.

Ridicule often checks what is absurd, and fully as often smothers that which is noble.

No one ever was a great poet, that applied himself much to anything else.

When I pray, coincidences happen, and when I don't, they don't.

The only way for a rich man to be healthy is by exercise and abstinence, to live as if he were poor.

Maxim #1626: Sir Winston Churchill

Short words are best and the old words when short are best of all.

Maxim #1627: Sir Winston Churchill

The truth is incontrovertible. Malice may attack it. Ignorance may deride it. But in the end, there it is.

Maxim #1628: Sir Winston Churchill

Socialism is like a dream. Sooner or later you wake up to reality.

Maxim #1629: Sir Winston Churchill

When the eagles are silent the parrots begin to jabber.

Maxim #1630: Sir Winston Churchill

There is no worse mistake in public leadership than to hold out false hope soon to be swept away.

Maxim #1631: Sir Winston Churchill

We owe something to extravagance, for thrift and adventure seldom go hand in hand.

Maxim #1632: Sir Winston Churchill

I am ready to meet my Maker. Whether my Maker is prepared for the great ordeal of meeting me is another matter.

Victory is the beautiful, bright-colored flower. Transport is the stem without which it could never have blossomed.

Without tradition, art is a flock of sheep without a shepherd. Without innovation, it is a corpse.

To improve is to change; to be perfect is to change often.

Sure I am of this, that you have only to endure to conquer. You have only to persevere to save yourselves.

Politics are almost as exciting as war, and quite as dangerous. In war you can only be killed once, but in politics many times.

The inherent vice of capitalism is the unequal sharing of blessings; the inherent virtue of socialism is the equal sharing of miseries.

There is only one good -- knowledge; and only one evil -- ignorance.

The fewer our wants the more we resemble the Gods.

The nearest way to glory is to strive to be what you wish to be thought to be.

The way to gain a good reputation is to endeavor to be what you desire to appear.

Chide a friend in private and praise him in public.

There is no witness so terrible and no accuser so powerful as conscience which dwells within us.

Rather fail with honor than succeed by fraud.

Maxim #1646: Sophocles

The gods plant reason in mankind, of all good gifts the highest.

Maxim #1647: Sophocles

Wisdom is the supreme part of happiness.

Maxim #1648: Soren Kierkegaard

Life is not a problem to be solved, but a reality to be experienced.

Maxim #1649: Soren Kierkegaard

What our age lacks is not reflection, but passion.

Maxim #1650: Source Unknown

The smallest good deed is better than the grandest intention

Maxim #1651: Spanish Proverb

Who has a trade may go anywhere.

Maxim #1652: Spanish Proverb

Take what you want, God said to man, and pay for it.

Maxim #1653: Sri Swami Sivananda

Put your heart, mind, intellect and soul even to your smallest acts. This is the secret of success.

Maxim #1654: St. Augustine

To abstain from sin when one can no longer sin is to be forsaken by sin, not to forsake it.

Maxim #1655: St. Augustine

This is the very perfection of a man, to find out his own imperfections.

Maxim #1656: St. Augustine

To many, total abstinence is easier than perfect moderation.

Maxim #1657: St. Augustine

Pray as though everything depended on God. Work as though everything depended on you.

Maxim #1658: St. Gregory The Great

The universe is not rich enough to buy the vote of an honest man.

Maxim #1659: Stanley C. Gault

We don't work for each other, We work with each other.

Maxim #1660: Sterling W. Sill

The way of success is not run with seven league boots but step by step, little by little, bit by bit...with no exceptions allowed.

Maxim #1661: Steve Bubinstein

Women speak two languages - one of which is verbal.

Maxim #1662: Steve Jobs

Sometimes when you innovate, you make mistakes. It is best to admit them quickly, and get on with improving your other innovations.

Maxim #1663: Steve Mayham

This is an industry of ideas and imagination, and what we are selling is hope.

Maxim #1664: Steve Miller

The question to everyone's answer is usually asked from within.

Maxim #1665: Steve Schmidt

The price for independence is often isolation and solitude.

Maxim #1666: Steven Wright

You can't have everything. Where would you put it?

Maxim #1667: Stewart Udall

We have, I fear, confused power with greatness.

Maxim #1668: Stuart Chase

Sanely applied advertising could remake the world.

Maxim #1669: Sun Tzu

Strategy without tactics is the slowest route to victory. Tactics without strategy is the noise before defeat.

Maxim #1670: Susan Faludi

Women are enslaved by their own liberation.

Maxim #1671: Susan Taylor

We don't have an eternity to realize our dreams, only the time we are here.

Maxim #1672: Swedish Proverb.

Sweep first before your own door, before you sweep the doorsteps of your neighbors.

Shared joy is double joy and shared sorrow is half-sorrow.

Those who imagine that the world is against them have generally conspired to make it true.

To love and be loved is the great happiness of existence.

Where is the wisdom we have lost in knowledge? Where is the knowledge we have lost in information.

Only by acceptance of the past, can you alter it.

We shall not cease from exploration and the end of all our exploring will be to arrive where we started... and know the place for the first time.

When the state is most corrupt, then the laws are most multiplied.

Maxim #1680: Taisen Deshimaru

To receive everything, one must open one's hands and give.

Maxim #1681: Tecumseh

When the legends die, the dreams end; there is no more greatness.

Maxim #1682: Telegraph Magazine

Whoever says money can't buy you happiness doesn't know where to shop.

Maxim #1683: Terrence

When we cannot act as we wish, we must act as we can.

Maxim #1684: Terry Bradshaw

What's the worst thing that can happen to a quarterback? He loses his confidence.

Maxim #1685: The 14th Dalai Lama

The purpose of our lives is to be happy.

Maxim #1686: The Talmud

Loving kindness is greater than laws; and the charities of life are more than all ceremonies.

Maxim #1687: The Talmud

Who is wise? One who learns from all.

Maxim #1688: The Talmud

This is the punishment of a liar: he is not believed, even when he speaks the truth.

Maxim #1689: The Talmud

The end result of wisdom is... good deeds.

Maxim #1690: Themistocles

The Athenians govern the Greeks; I govern the Athenians; you, my wife, govern me; your son governs you.

Maxim #1691: Theodore Leavitt

The purpose of business is to create and keep a customer.

Maxim #1692: Theodore Parker

Self-denial is indispensable to a strong character, and the highest kind comes from a religious stock.

Maxim #1693: Theodore Parker

The books that help you the most are those which make you think the most.

Maxim #1694: Theodore Roethke

Time marks us while we are marking time.

Maxim #1695: Theodore Roosevelt

This country will not be a good place for any of us to live in unless we make it a good place for all of us to live in.

Maxim #1696: Theodore Roosevelt

The first requisite of a good citizen in this Republic of ours is that he shall be able and willing to pull his weight.

Maxim #1697: Theodore Roosevelt

What I am to be, I am becoming.

Maxim #1698: Theodosia Garrison

The hardest habit of all to break is the terrible habit of happiness.

Maxim #1699: Thomas A. Edison

The first requisite for success is the ability to apply your physical and mental energies to one problem incessantly without growing weary.

Maxim #1700: Thomas A. Edison

Restlessness is discontent and discontent is the first necessity of progress. Show me a thoroughly satisfied man and I will show you a failure.

Maxim #1701: Thomas A. Edison

The value of an idea lies in the using of it.

Maxim #1702: Thomas A. Edison

When I have fully decided that a result is worth getting I go ahead of it and make trial after trial until it comes.

Maxim #1703: Thomas A. Edison

Show me a thoroughly satisfied man and I will show you a failure.

Maxim #1704: Thomas A. Kempis

We usually know what we can do, but temptation shows us who we are.

Maxim #1705: Thomas Alva Edison

The inventor tries to meet the demand of a crazy civilization.

Maxim #1706: Thomas Brooks

God hears no more than the heart speaks; and if the heart be dumb, God will certainly be deaf.

Maxim #1707: Thomas C. Haliburton

Punctuality is the soul of business.

Maxim #1708: Thomas C. Haliburton

The happiness of every country depends upon the character of its people, rather than the form of its government.

Maxim #1709: Thomas Carlyle

The end of man is action, and not thought, though it be of the noblest.

Maxim #1710: Thomas Carlyle

Nothing is more terrible than activity without insight.

Maxim #1711: Thomas Carlyle

Everywhere in life, the true question is not what we gain, but what we do.

Maxim #1712: Thomas Carlyle

Our main business is not to see what lies dimly in the distance, but to do what lies clearly at hand.

Maxim #1713: Thomas Carlyle

The merit of originality is not novelty; it is sincerity.

Tell a man he is brave, and you help him to become so.

One must verify or expel his doubts, and convert them into the certainty of Yes or NO.

Vows are made in storms and forgotten in calm weather.

Thought would destroy their paradise.

Time changes everything except something within us which is always surprised by change.

Patience and tenacity of purpose are worth more than twice their weight of cleverness.

Time, whose tooth gnaws away at everything else, is powerless against truth.

The rung of a ladder was never meant to rest upon, but only to hold a man's foot long enough to enable him to put the other somewhat higher.

Wisdom is the power to put our time and our knowledge to the proper use.

We progress because we are willing to change.

How much pain worries have cost us that have never happened?

The only thing a man can take beyond this lifetime is his ethics.

The will of the people is the only legitimate foundation of any government, and to protect its free expression should be our first object.

Speeches that are measured by the hour will die with the hour.

Maxim #1728: Thomas Jefferson

The world is indebted for all triumphs which have been gained by reason and humanity over error and oppression.

Maxim #1729: Thomas Jefferson

Those who bear equally the burdens of government should equally participate in the benefits.

Maxim #1730: Thomas Jefferson

There is no truth existing which I fear, or would wish unknown to the whole world.

Maxim #1731: Thomas Jefferson

To compel a man to furnish contributions of money for the propagation of opinions which he disbelieves and abhors is sinful and tyrannical.

Maxim #1732: Thomas Jefferson

When angry, count ten before you speak; if very angry, count a hundred.

Maxim #1733: Thomas Jefferson

The most valuable of all talents is that of never using two words when one will do.

Maxim #1734: Thomas Jefferson

The happiest moments of my life have been the few which I have passed at home in the bosom of my family.

Maxim #1735: Thomas Jefferson

The man who fears no truth has nothing to fear from lies.

Maxim #1736: Thomas Mann

Opinions cannot survive if one has no chance to fight for them.

Maxim #1737: Thomas Morell

The first great gift we can bestow on others is a good example.

Maxim #1738: Thomas Paine

What we may obtain too cheap, we esteem too lightly: 't is dearness only that gives every thing its value.

Maxim #1739: Thomas Paine

When we are planning for posterity, we ought to remember that virtue is not hereditary.

Society in every state is a blessing, but Government, even in its best state, is but a necessary evil; in its worst state, an intolerable one.

What we obtain too cheap, we esteem too lightly; it is dearness only that gives everything its value.

People often say that this or that person has not yet found himself. But the self is not something that one finds. It is something one creates.

WE ARE NOT PUT INTO THIS WORLD TO SIT STILL AND KNOW; WE ARE PUT INTO IT TO ACT.

Women who seek to be equal with men lack ambition.

You can employ men and hire hands to work for you, but you must win their hearts to have them work with you.

Tolerance and celebration of individual differences is the fire that fuels lasting love.

To live happily with other people one should ask of them only what they can give.

To waken interest and kindle enthusiasm is the sure way to teach easily and successfully.

To rule one's anger is well; to prevent it is better.

The church is so subnormal that if it ever got back to the New Testament normal it would seem to people to be abnormal.

There is an abiding beauty which may be appreciated by those who will see things as they are and who will ask for no reward except to see.

Happy the man who knows the causes of things.

They can because they think they can.

We are slaves to whatever we don't understand

Truth is not a matter of personal viewpoint.

Success is as ice cold and lonely as the North Pole.

People do not lack strength, they lack will.

Success is always temporary. When all is said and one, the only thing you'll have left is your character.

Individual commitment to a group effort - that is what makes a team work, a company work, a society work, a civilization work.

The quality of a man's life is in direct proportion to his commitment to excellence, regardless of his chosen field of endeavor.

The spirit, the will to win, and the will to excel are the things that endure. These qualities are so much more important than the events that occur.

Winning is a habit. Unfortunately, so is losing.

Still, there is a calm, pure harmony, and music inside of me.

Trust one who has tried.

You can never correct your work well until you have forgotten it.

Maxim #1766: Voltaire

Work banishes those three great evils: boredom, vice and poverty.

Maxim #1767: Voltaire

The discovery of what is true, and the practice of that which is good, are the two most important objects of philosophy.

Maxim #1768: W. Clement Stone

If there is something to gain and nothing to lose by asking, by all means ask!

Maxim #1769: W. Clement Stone

No matter how carefully you plan your goals they will never be more than pipe dreams unless you pursue them with gusto.

Maxim #1770: W. Fusselman

Today a reader, tomorrow a leader.

Maxim #1771: W. S. Gilbert

You have no idea what a poor opinion I have of myself; and how little I deserve it.

Maxim #1772: W. Somerset Maugham

Old age has its pleasures, which, though different, are not less than the pleasures of youth.

It is unfair to expect a politician to live in private up to the statements he makes in public.

Old age is ready to undertake tasks that youth shirked because they would take too long.

You know what the critics are. If you tell the truth they only say you're cynical and it does an author no good to get a reputation for cynicism.

Nothing endures but personal qualities.

To me every hour of the light and dark is a miracle. Every cubic inch of space is a miracle.

There is no week nor day nor hour when tyranny may not enter upon this country, if the people lose their roughness and spirit of defiance.

The shallow consider liberty a release from all law, from every constraint. The wise man sees in it, on the contrary, the potent Law of Laws.

Whatever satisfies the soul is truth.

The whole history of civilization is strewn with creeds and institutions which were invaluable at first, and deadly afterwards.

To be happy is to be able to become aware of oneself without fright.

Our job is only to hold up the mirror -- to tell and show the public what has happened.

Rabbi Zusya said that on the Day of Judgment, God would ask him, not why he had not been Moses, but why he had not been Zusya.

Maxim #1785: Walter Lippmann

The first principle of a civilized state is that the power is legitimate only when it is under contract.

Maxim #1786: Walter Pater

To burn always with this hard, gem-like flame, to maintain this ecstasy, is success in life.

Maxim #1787: Walter Savage Landor

The writing of the wise are the only riches our posterity cannot squander.

Maxim #1788: Walter de La Mare

Too late for fruit, too soon for flowers.

Maxim #1789: Warren Buffett

If a business does well, the stock eventually follows.

Maxim #1790: Warren Buffett

Risk comes from not knowing what you're doing.

Maxim #1791: Washington Irving

The natural principle of war is to do the most harm to our enemy with the least harm to ourselves; and this of course is to be effected by stratagem.

Maxim #1792: Washington Irving

The tongue is the only instrument that gets sharper with use.

Maxim #1793: Wayne Dyer

There's no scarcity of opportunity to make a living at what you love. There is only a scarcity of resolve to make it happen.

Maxim #1794: Wayne Dyer

People who want the most approval get the least and people who need approval the least get the most.

Maxim #1795: Webster's Duchess of Malp.

There is not in nature a thing that makes a man so deform'd, so beastly, as doth intemperate anger.

Maxim #1796: Wendell Lewis Wilkie

Whenever we take away the liberties of those whom we hate we are opening the way to loss of liberty for those we love.

Maxim #1797: Wendell Phillips

To be as good as our fathers we must be better, imitation is not discipleship

Maxim #1798: Westbrook Pegler

I am a member of the rabble in good standing.

Maxim #1799: Whole Earth Catalog

We ARE as gods and might as well get good at it.

Maxim #1800: Will Rogers

Ancient Rome declined because it had a Senate; now what's going to happen to us with both a Senate and a House?

Maxim #1801: Will Rogers

"Even if you're on the right track, you'll get run over if you just sit there."

Maxim #1802: Will Rogers

Strangers are just friends I haven't met yet.

Maxim #1803: Will Rogers

We'd all vote for the best man, but he's never a candidate.

Maxim #1804: William Arthur Ward

When we seek to discover the best in others, we somehow bring out the best in ourselves.

A dog starved at his master's gate Predicts the ruin of the state.

To generalize is to be an idiot. To particularize is the alone distinction of merit. General knowledge are those knowledge that idiots possess.

Without contraries is no progression. Attraction and repulsion, reason and energy, love and hate, are necessary to human existence.

The more you learn what to do with yourself, and the more you do for others, the more you will learn to enjoy the abundant life.

A self-made man? Yes, and one who worships his creator.

A fool must now and then be right, by chance.

Maxim #1811: William Crashaw

When human power becomes so great and original that we can account for it only as a kind of divine imagination, we call it genius.

Maxim #1812: William Ellery Channing

All noble enthusiasms pass through a feverish stage, and grow wiser and more serene.

Maxim #1813: William Faulkner

The man who removes a mountain begins by carrying away small stones.

Maxim #1814: William Hazlitt

Those who can command themselves command others.

Maxim #1815: William Hazlitt

Those who make their dress a principal part of themselves will, in general, become of no more value than their dress.

Maxim #1816: William Hazlitt

Prosperity is a great teacher; adversity a greater.

Maxim #1817: William Hazlitt

To give a reason for anything is to breed a doubt of it.

Maxim #1818: William Hazlitt

The player envies only the player, the poet envies only the poet.

Maxim #1819: William Hazlitt

We can scarcely hate anyone that we know.

Maxim #1820: William J. H. Boetcker

You cannot establish security on borrowed money.

Maxim #1821: William James

Our belief at the beginning of a doubtful undertaking is the one thing that insures the successful outcome of our venture.

Maxim #1822: William James

The greatest discovery of my generation is that human beings can alter their lives by altering their attitudes of mind.

Maxim #1823: William James

The deepest craving in human nature is the craving to be appreciated.

We never fully grasp the import of any true statement until we have a clear notion of what the opposite untrue statement would be.

The highest happiness on earth is marriage. Every man who is happily married is a successful man even if he has failed in everything else.

There will be no peace so long as God remains unseated at the conference table.

A good laugh is sunshine in the house.

Kindnesses are easily forgotten; but injuries! -- what worthy man does not keep those in mind?

There is no good in living in a society where you are merely the equal of everybody else. The true pleasure of life is to live with your inferiors.

Will is character in action.

Maxim #1831: William Mcgovern

The fact that it had never been done before made it even more irresistible.

Maxim #1832: William Mcgovern

The only practice that's now constant is the practice of constantly accommodating to change.

Maxim #1833: William Morris Hughes

Without the Empire we should be tossed like a cork in the cross current of world politics. It is at once our sword and our shield.

Maxim #1834: William Penn

Right is right, even if everyone is against it; and wrong is wrong, even if everyone is for it.

Maxim #1835: William Penn

We have a call to do good, as often as we have the power and occasion.

Maxim #1836: William Pitt

Poverty, of course, is no disgrace, but it is damned annoying.

Maxim #1837: William R. Alger

The wealth of a soul is measured by how much it can feel; its poverty by how little.

Proverbs are mental gems gathered in the diamond fields of the mind.

We must remember that a right lost to one is lost to all.

I will praise any man that will praise me.

I can get no remedy against this consumption of the purse: borrowing only lingers and lingers it out, but the disease is incurable.

Patch grief with proverbs.

I care not, a man can die but once; we owe God and death.

No legacy is so rich as honestly.

Things won are done, joy's soul lies in the doing.

'Tis the mind that makes the body rich.

Wise men never sit and wail their loss, but cheerily seek how to redress their harms.

The very firstlings of my heart shall be The firstlings of my hand.

They say men are molded out of faults, and for the most, become much more the better; for being a little bad. [Measure For Measure]

'Tis an ill cook that cannot lick his own fingers.

Things done well and with a care, exempt themselves from fear.

Maxim #1852: William Shakespeare

There is nothing good or bad, but thinking makes it so.

Maxim #1853: William Shakespeare

We know what we are, but know not what we may be.

Maxim #1854: William Shenstone

A liar begins with making falsehood appear like truth, and ends with making truth itself appear like falsehood.

Maxim #1855: William Somerset Maugham

Tradition is a guide and not a jailer.

Maxim #1856: William T. Cummings

There are no atheists in foxholes.

Maxim #1857: William Temple

The only for a rich man to be healthy is by exercise and abstinence, to live as if he were poor.

Maxim #1858: William Wordsworth

That best portion of a good man's life; His little, nameless, unremembered acts of kindness and of love.

The child is the father of the man.

When you're riding, only the race in which you're riding is important.

The worst tempered people I have ever met were those who knew that they were wrong.

Some rob you with a six-gun and some with a fountain pen.

There is a price which is too great to pay for peace, and that price can be put in one word. One cannot pay the price of self-respect.

You cannot hold your head high with your hand out.

So sure are you! Tried have you? Always with you it cannot be done. Hear you nothing that I say? Try not. Do! Do! Or do not. There is no try.

To know and not to do is not yet to know.

Success is the maximum utilization of the ability that you have.

You have to "be" before you can "do," and do before you can "have."

Success and happiness are not destinations, they are exciting, never-ending journeys.

Positive thinking will let you do everything better than negative thinking will.

Winning is not everything, but the effort to win is.

The most important persuasion tool you have in your entire arsenal is integrity.

Take care to be an economist in prosperity; there is no fear of your not being one in adversity.

How To Use This Book

Why on earth would anyone place a section describing how to use a book, at the end of the book?

So we can see how many pages it has!

Why should anyone (next to a publisher at least) *care* about how many pages are a book?

--Because there is nothing more boring that reading a lot of quotes at once!

After gleaning that page / maxim number from the previous page, feel free to read the *next* few ideas on how to put that bit of trivia, to good use!

The Way of the Numbers

Unless you suffer from insomnia (yet another way reading quotes can help us ;-), then here is an idea of how to read any collection of thoughts:

Do you have anything that can generate a number between 1 and the number of pages in this book? If so, then use it to generate two numbers - One between one and the page count. Yet another between 1 and 10 or 12.

After you have those two numbers, use the "page roll" to take you to a page in this book. Then use that *second* number to help you find your "quote for today." (If that second numbers leads you past page or the number of quotes in the book, then simply start reading at the beginning of the next page / book, again.)

The Way of the Coins

If you do not have a way to generate random numbers, I used to recommend using a handful of coins. Now that we've almost 2,000 maxims, coin-tossing is no longer practical.

Rather than chumming tails then, why not consider using something like the Python programming language? A planetary phenomenon, the Python programming language ("Python") is both free & available from python.**org**.

In our case:

```
#!/usr/bin/env python3
import random
pop = 1873
print("Maxim Number:",
    random.randrange(1, pop+1))
```

Because Python is presently available upon ever popular computing system known to humanity, you might be surprised how readily the programming language can be used to solve many commonplace chores.

While difficult to master, Python is also the easiest 'tech to learn when we simply need to get things done (like generating random numbers :) quickly.

I've also lots of <u>free training</u> to help you get started using the Python, as well as other technologies, at places like Udemy. See https://www.udemy.com/user/randallnagy2/ for the ever-growing list?

Other Ways

We can also just randomly open this book to let our attention latch onto any interesting quote. That is what I usually do.

Finally, some quote enthusiasts also use my "Doctor Quote" software, mentioned previously. Because Doctor Quote has tens of thousands of quotations in it, the software also provides a "surprise me" quotation query, as well. Through the miracle of Microsoft Windows emulation, we can even use Doctor Quote on Linux, as well.

p.s. 'Blushingly rated as a 5-Star Shareware Product by PC WEEK and many other software reviewers, for the past few decades the program has evolved to enjoy well over 2,500 downloads a month.

Thanks for reading,

-Randall Nagy